2nd Edition

GCE A Level Economics

The Examination Skills Guide

2nd Edition

GCE A Level Economics

The Examination Skills Guide

CHRISTABELLE SOH

World Scientific

NEW JERSEY • LONDON • SINGAPORE • BEIJING • SHANGHAI • HONG KONG • TAIPEI • CHENNAI • TOKYO

Published by

World Scientific Publishing Co. Pte. Ltd.
5 Toh Tuck Link, Singapore 596224
USA office: 27 Warren Street, Suite 401-402, Hackensack, NJ 07601
UK office: 57 Shelton Street, Covent Garden, London WC2H 9HE

National Library Board, Singapore Cataloguing in Publication Data
Name(s): Soh, Christabelle.
Title: GCE A level economics : the examination skills guide / Christabelle Soh.
Description: Second edition. | Singapore : World Scientific Publishing Co. Pte. Ltd., [2023]
Identifier(s): ISBN 978-981-12-7478-7 (hardcover) | 978-981-12-7498-5 (paperback) |
978-981-12-7479-4 (ebook for institutions) | 978-981-12-7480-0 (ebook for individuals)
Subject(s): LCSH: Economics--Examinations--Study guides. |
Economics--Examinations, questions, etc.
Classification: DDC 330.076--dc23

British Library Cataloguing-in-Publication Data
A catalogue record for this book is available from the British Library.

For any available supplementary material, please visit
https://www.worldscientific.com/worldscibooks/10.1142/13367#t=suppl

Desk Editor: Nicole Ong

Typeset by Diacritech Technologies Pvt. Ltd.
Chennai - 600106, India

About the Author

Christabelle Soh is the former Subject Head of Economics at Millennia Institute. Her time as an educator started with her first job as an Economics tutor at Raffles Institution. She then had a stint as an evaluative studies officer at the Ministry of Education's Headquarters (MOEHQ) before being posted to Millennia Institute.

Outside of formal work, Christabelle is an editor of *Economics & Society*, a publication under the Economic Society of Singapore. She has also authored and co-authored articles that have been published in Singapore's national newspapers and contributed chapters to books on Economics. Her publications cover a range of economic issues, from a game-theoretic approach to the Southeast Asia transboundary haze problem to the concept of an optimal population size that balances economic growth with qualitative aspects of standard of living.

Prior to joining the labour force, Christabelle majored in Economics at Nanyang Technological University of Singapore (NTU). She graduated with First Class Honours and received the Ministry of Trade and Industry (MTI) Economist Service Book Prize, the Koh Boon Hwee University Scholar's Award, and the Lee Kuan Yew Gold Medal. She was also an NTU President Research Scholar for the years in which she was eligible. Christabelle's two great passions are Economics and Education. She is currently marrying both passions by pursuing a Master's Degree in Economics.

Contents

Chapter 1
Introduction

1.1 The Performance Formula

Over the course of my years in teaching, I have had the privilege of working with a wide range of students. Most students work hard, but not all who work hard perform well in examinations. There are many possible reasons for this. Students could have used poor study techniques such that the many hours spent still resulted in them not learning very much. Or, they might have started too late and therefore did not manage to complete their revision. There could also be examination anxiety and other psychological obstacles. And then, you have the cases where the students have put in the hard work, clearly understood the content, entered the examination hall with confidence, and still performed below expectations. Why then, do these not perform well?

The reason is surprisingly simple. There are two ingredients that students need to do well in the GCE A Level Examinations for Economics — content mastery and Economics-specific examination skills. Students who have revised the content thoroughly could still perform poorly because they lack the latter. How economic content and examination skills determine results can be represented by the following formula:

$$\text{Content} \times \text{Skills} = \text{Results.}$$

Content would refer to the percentage of the testable content that a student knows (i.e., if you only know half of the concepts tested in the A Level examinations, your content would be 50%). Skills refer to the percentage of examination skills required for the A Level examinations such as question analysis skills. If you only know half the required skills, then your skills would be 50%.

The intuition behind the formula is this — content represents how much you know of the economic concepts and skills represent how well you can use these concepts to meet the requirements of the examination questions. So, if you know all the concepts (100% for content) but can only apply them correctly to meet question requirements about half the time (50% for skills), then naturally you would only get half the marks. This is because for half the questions, you know the questions requirements and have the necessary content to answer it. So, you will earn the marks for this half of the questions. For the other half of the questions, however, you do not even know what is required and hence gain no marks. This gives you an overall result of 50% of the marks. Mathematically, we can represent it as 100% for content × 50% for skills = 50% for results. Conversely, if you know half the concepts (50% for content) but, are able to meet the question requirements perfectly for the questions that test these concepts (100% for skills), then you would also get half the marks as you would score perfectly for the half of the questions that test the concepts you know but nothing on the questions that test the concepts you do not know (50% × 100% = 50%). We can also represent this intuition diagrammatically.

In Figure 1.1, the lighter the background, the better the results and the darker the background, the poorer the results. Students need high percentages of both content and skills to do well. Assuming an A grade requires a result of 70%, a student would need about 85% of the content and 85% of the skills to obtain an A grade (85% × 85% = 72.25%).[1]

Figure 1.1: The performance formula represented diagrammatically.

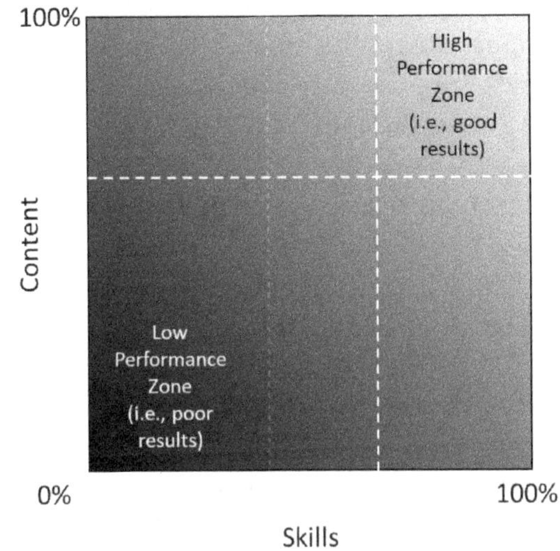

1.2 How Much You Will Benefit From This Book

If you understand the performance formula, then you will also realise that this book, which teaches examination skills, creates the largest benefit for students who already have most of the content. Let us illustrate this with a numerical example.

Let us imagine that there are two students — Ash and Brook. Ash knows 100% of the content and only 40% of the skills. Brook knows 70% of the content and similarly, also only has 40% of the skills. If they both improve their skills by 10 percentage points (i.e., now they both have 50% of the skills), Ash's results would improve by 10 percentage points $((100\% \times 50\%) - (100\% \times 40\%) = 10\%)$ whereas Brook's results would only improve by 7 percentage points $((70\% \times 50\%) - (70\% \times 40\%) = 7\%)$. In other words, the more content you already know, the greater the gains in results you will obtain from learning the skills from this book. This is because the skills help you to apply the content to meet the question requirements. If you lack the content to begin with, naturally it will not make much difference.

Having said that, if you pick up the skills first, every extra bit of content that you pick up after that creates a greater bang for your buck in terms of examination results. Again, let us illustrate this with a numerical example. Suppose Ash and Brook had the same starting point of knowing 50% of the content and 40% of the skills. If Ash picks up more skills such that she now has 50% of the skills, then every 10 percentage point increment in content that she gains would translate into a 5 percentage point improvement in results (e.g., (60% × 50%) – (50% × 50%) = 5%) whereas for Brook, the equivalent figure would only be 4 percentage points (e.g., (60% × 40%) – (50% × 40%) = 4%).

In summary, the more content you already have, the more an improvement in skills would improve your results. And, the more skills you have, the more an increase in content you know would improve your results. If you have neither in this moment, breathe, and start working on picking up both.

1.3 How to Use This Book

This book is organised into two sections. The first section covers the skills needed to answer case study questions and the second section covers the skills needed to answer essay questions. Each section is then divided into chapters that cover a specific skill each (refer to the Contents page to see what the specific skills are). In each chapter, the skill covered is illustrated using worked examples of examination-type questions. And, at the end of each section, a summary of the skills required is provided. A final chapter on strategies for tackling atypical questions rounds up the book.

If you have no idea what skills you lack (i.e., you do not know what you do not know), you can read this book cover to cover to cover all ground. Alternatively, you can use the diagnostic tool in Table 1.1 to guide you in discovering what it is that you do not know.

On the other hand, if you already know which skills you lack specifically (i.e., you know what you do not know), you can select the relevant chapter(s) to read as each chapter is written such that it can be

Table 1.1: Diagnostic tool to determine what you do not know.

If you...	You lack...
Get lost in the case study extracts and do not know what the main points of the extracts are is	Reading skills (read Chapter 3)
Frequently misinterpret numerical data in the case material (e.g., numbers in tables/charts/figures)	Numerical interpretation skills (read Chapter 4)
Understand the case material and know the content but cannot seem to score well	Answering skills for case studies (look at your tests to see which types of questions you tend to score poorly in (e.g., always scoring poorly for "discuss" questions) and read the relevant section in Chapter 5)
(For H2 only) Score poorly for essays	Answering skills for essays (read Chapter 7)
Know what the question is asking for but lack the content knowledge to answer it	Content knowledge (this book will not help you very much)

understood on its own.[2] The summary at the end of each section is especially useful as a revision tool for a quick refresher of the skills before you take the relevant papers (for H2 Economics (9570 syllabus), Paper 1 is the case study paper and will require skills from Section 1 of this book while Paper 2 is the essay paper and will require skills from Section 2 of this book. For H1 Economics (8843 syllabus), there is only one paper — the case study paper. This will require skills from Section 1 of this book).

If you are taking the H1 Economics (8843 syllabus) examination, you will find the first section (and the last chapter) useful. If you are taking the H2 Economics (9570 syllabus) examination, you will find the entire book useful.

Endnotes

1. Or, if you are more mathematically inclined, the square root of 70% gives 83.67%. So, having 83.76% of both content and skills would be enough for an A grade.
2. Note that this also means that there may be some repetition when there are overlaps.

Part 1
Case Study Skills

Chapter 2
The Structure of a Case Study Question

Before we jump into the examination skills, it is good to have the lay of the land (i.e., understand the structure of a case study question).

2.1 The H1 Economics Case Study Question (8843 Syllabus)

For this syllabus, there is only one 3-h paper. In this paper are two case study questions of 40 marks each. In each case study, there are typically 2–3 pages of case material (comprising both textual and numerical data, including graphs) and 7–8 part-questions. Part-questions are sub-questions. For example, questions 1(a) and 1(b) are two part-questions. 1(ai) and 1(aii) also constitute two part-questions (so 1(ai), 1(aii) and 1(b) would count as 3 part-questions). Of these questions, 3 part-questions will require higher-order thinking skills and carry about 24 marks (typically, one will carry 6 marks, another will carry 8 marks, and the last will carry 10 marks). These three questions can be identified by the command word used (see Figure 2.1). The remaining questions carry the remaining 16 marks and are generally simpler. Of these 16 marks, usually about 2 marks go towards numerical data description or comparison or calculation. All the above information is presented in Figure 2.1.

Figure 2.1: The structure of a H1 Economics Case Study Question.

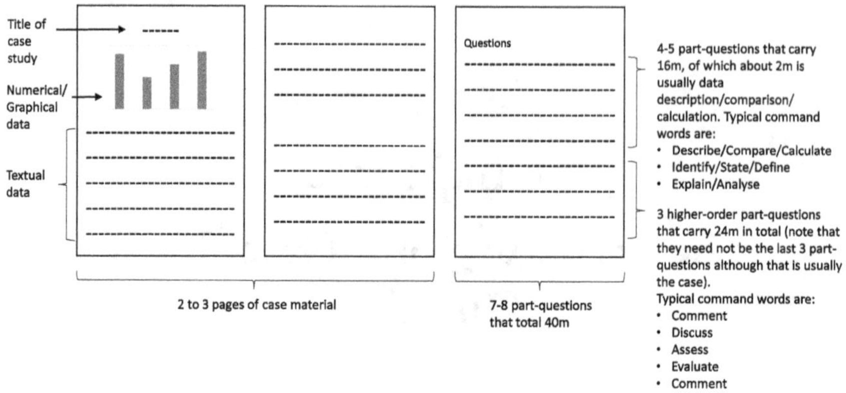

The part-questions that carry the 16 marks are marked by points, meaning to say that each mark is allocated to a specific point/thing that must be shown in the answer. In contrast, the 3 higher-order part-questions are marked by levels.[1] This means that instead of looking out for specific points, the answer is read as a whole, and then marked according to a rubric that describes the main features of a good answer and a poor answer. The specifics of how each type of question is marked and therefore how you ought to answer them will be explained in the subsequent pages under each of the command words in Chapter 5. (Please feel free to skip ahead. This book need not be read cover to cover.)

2.2 The H2 Economics Case Study Question (9570 Syllabus)

For this syllabus, Paper 1 is the case study paper (which constitutes 40% of the total score) and Paper 2 is the essay paper (which constitutes the other 60%). Paper 1 is a 2-h 15-min paper that comprises two case study questions of 30 marks each. In each case study, there are typically 2–3 pages of case material which consists of both textual and numerical data (including graphs) and 6–7 part-questions. Part-questions are sub-questions. For example, questions 1(a) and 1(b) are two part-questions. 1(ai) and 1(aii) also constitute two part-questions

Figure 2.2: The structure of a H2 Economics Case Study Question.

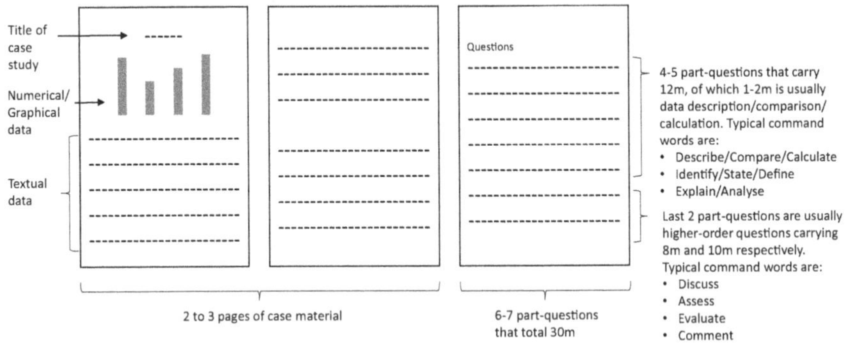

(so 1(ai), 1(aii) and 1(b) would count as 3 part-questions). Of these questions, 2 part-questions will test higher-order thinking and carry 18 marks (one will carry 8 marks and the other 10 marks). These are typically the last two questions and can be identified both by the command word used and the marks carried. The remaining questions carry the remaining 12 marks and are generally simpler. Of these 12 marks, usually about 1–2 marks go towards numerical data description or comparison or calculation. All the above is presented in Figure 2.2.

The 4–5 part-questions that carry the first 12 marks are marked by points. This means that each mark is allocated to a specific point/ thing that must be shown in the answer. In contrast, the last two higher-order part-questions are marked by levels. This means that instead of being screened for specific points, the answer is read as a whole, and then marked according to a rubric that describes the main features of a good answer and a poor answer. The specifics of how each type of question is marked and therefore how you ought to answer them will be explained in the subsequent pages under each of the command words in Chapter 5 (please feel free to skip ahead; this book need not be read cover to cover).

Endnote

1. The “Explain… and comment…” question type is the awkward exception, as you will discover in Chapter 5.

Chapter 3
Understanding the Case Material — Reading Skills

3.1 Introduction

In every case study question, there will be 2–3 pages of case study material before the questions. The case material will include both textual and numerical data (including graphs). Since the questions are based on the case study, it is important to understand the case material. Additionally, this must be accomplished within a short span of no more than 10 min per question to leave you with enough time to complete your answers. This chapter shows you the skills required to understand the textual data (i.e., reading skills) in the shortest amount of time.

3.2 Use the Case Study Question's Title to Determine the Question's Focus (Micro/Macro)

The first thing to read is the title of the entire case study question. This is usually found in the middle of the first page of the case study question (see Figure 3.1). This title usually carries clues to help you determine whether the case study questions will mainly test microeconomic or macroeconomic concepts. This then primes your brain for recalling the relevant content.

Titles that focus on specific industries (e.g., food, cigarettes, healthcare, education) tell you that the case study question is likely to be

Figure 3.1: Title of the case study question.

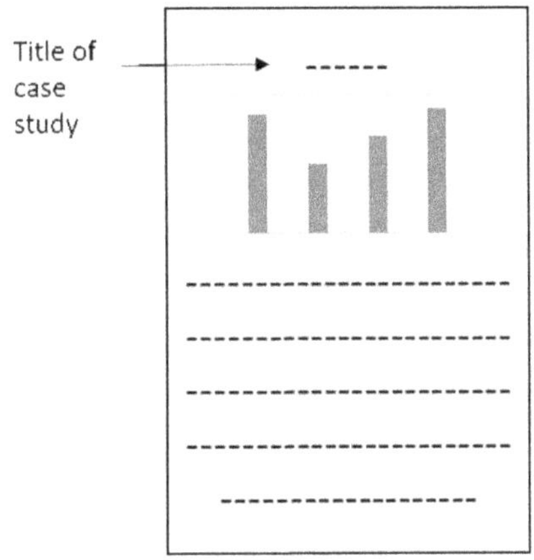

Table 3.1: Examples of case study question titles.

Possible Case Study Question Titles	Likely Focus	Likely Topics Tested
The 2008 food crisis *Healthcare systems around the world* *Issues with e-cigarettes and other products*	Microeconomics (since the titles show that the case studies are about specific markets)	• Demand and Supply • Elasticities • Market Structure (not in H1 Economics 8843 syllabus) • Market Failure • Microeconomic Policies
The Global Financial Crisis — 10 years on *Abenomics and the future of the Japanese economy* *Trade issues between US and China*	Macroeconomics (since the titles show that the case studies are about an economy or a few economies)	• Application of aggregate demand and supply • Macroeconomic aims, issues, and policies • Globalisation (not in H1 Economics 8843 syllabus)

microeconomics-based whereas titles that focus on a country(s) or an economy(s) tell you that the case study question is likely to be macroeconomics-based. Table 3.1 shows some examples of possible case study titles, whether it is likely to be a microeconomics/

macroeconomics-focussed case study question, and the likely topics that will be tested.

There are two caveats that must be made here. The first caveat is that well-set case studies would have sensible titles that summarise the issues and hence would be of use to you. However, case studies are not necessarily always well-set. In fact, while the A Level Examination Case Study Papers always provide titles for each case study question, internal examinations in schools may not always do so. As such, if the title is missing or makes little sense to you, ignore it and move on (remember, time is of the essence). The second caveat is that sometimes the case study question could include both microeconomic and macroeconomic elements. As such, even after you establish the focus of the case study question, you would still need to do the question analysis of each part-question (covered in Chapter 5) to determine whether microeconomic or macroeconomic content is required.

3.3 Getting the Key Information from Each Extract

Apart from the title, the other textual data provided in a case study question appears in the form of extracts from real-world sources such as news articles. The length of each extract varies from a short paragraph of a few lines to a full-page article with multiple paragraphs. An example of an extract is shown in Box 3.1. Instead of drowning in the details, it is imperative to get the key information from each extract accurately and efficiently. As such, you should do the following:

- Read the extract title to anchor your brain;
- Ignore numbers and focus on economic variables;
- Annotate cause-and-effect relationships;
- Summarise lists.

While the structure of a book necessitates going through each bullet point in a stepwise manner, the second to fourth bullet points ought to be done simultaneously when reading the extracts.

Box 3.1: Example of a case study extract.

> **Extract 1: China exports rebound in April, but outlook remains grim**
>
> China's exports unexpectedly rose in April for the first time this year as factories raced to make up for lost sales due to the coronavirus shock, but a double-digit fall in imports signals more trouble ahead as the global economy sinks into recession.
>
> Overseas shipments in April rose 3.5 per cent from a year earlier, marking the first positive growth since December last year, customs data showed on Thursday. The increase was driven in part by rising exports of medical equipment, traditional Chinese medicine and textiles, which include masks. China exported millions of tonnes of medical products worth 71.2 billion yuan (S$14.2 billion) in the March–April period, according to the customs agency. The daily export value of medical supplies jumped by more than three times last month.
>
> Some economists also attributed the rise in exports to factory closures elsewhere, leading to a surge in import demand, just as China's manufacturers reopened after extended shutdowns due to the virus outbreak.
>
> In light of the rebound in April shipments, Nomura raised its forecasts for China's exports to minus 22 per cent for May and June from minus 30 per cent previously, but still deep in contraction as the coronavirus crisis ravages the global economy.
>
> *Source*: *The Straits Times*, 7 May 2020. Retrieved on 15 May 2020 from: https://www.straitstimes.com/business/economy/china-exports-see-surprise-gain-in-april-but-rebound-seen-as-temporary

3.3.1 *Read the extract's title to anchor your brain*

First, read the title of each extract before you read the extract. This may seem to be silly advice, but I have encountered students who, in the interest of time, decided to skip reading extract titles to "save time". This is a poor decision because the extract title tells you what the extract is about. As such, it anchors your brain and allows faster processing of the extract's information. To illustrate the point of anchoring helping to improve your brain's processing speed, we will use a well-known illustration from the field of psychology.

Read the following passage from Bransford & Johnson (1972) and see how well you can process what is happening.

> *A newspaper is better than a magazine. A seashore is a better than the street. At first, it is better to run than to walk. You may have to try several times. It takes some skill but it is easy to learn. Even young children can enjoy it. Once successful, complications are minimal. Birds seldom get too close. Rain, however, soaks in very fast. Too many people doing the same thing can cause problems. One needs lots of room. If there are no complications, it can be very peaceful. A rock will serve as an anchor. If things break loose from it, however, you will not get a second chance.*

Confused?

You should be. Now imagine that you are told that the title of the paragraph is "Making and flying a kite". Read the paragraph again. Isn't it much easier to understand now?

The researchers who came up with this example showed that when people were provided with the title before they read the paragraph, their comprehension and recall were much better than those who were not provided the title or were provided the title later. Of course, this paragraph has been manipulated to remove all hints and mentions of the word "kite" and is an extreme example of the usefulness of titles. Nonetheless, the main point is still valid — reading the extract titles first will help you save precious processing time.

If we use the sample extract in Box 3.1, the title "China exports rebound in April, but outlook remains grim" immediately tells us what Extract 1 is about — that Chinese exports have risen but are not expected to continue to do so. So, when you start reading the extract, your brain will easily process the points as causes of the rebound or why the outlook remains grim, etc.

Again, the caveat holds — if the case study is not well-set, the extract's title may not be useful. In such cases, ignore it and move on.

3.3.2 *Ignore numbers and focus on economic variables*

Once you start reading the actual extract, skim. You want to ignore specific numbers and focus on the economic variables. Now what do we mean by economic variables? Economic variables are the things we study in economic models. This includes both the dependent and independent variables. Dependent variables are the variables whose values depend on other variables and independent variables are the variables whose values determine the value of the dependent variable(s). For example, in the demand and supply model, economic variables would include the price of a good and its quantity traded (which are the dependent variables as their values are dependent on other variables), as well as things like the income of consumers, the price of substitutes/complements, the cost of production, etc. (which are the independent variables as they determine the values of the price and quantity traded). Table 3.2 provides more examples of economic variables from a microeconomic model and macroeconomic model. Note that you do not need to memorise the definitions of dependent and independent variables. It is helpful, however, to know what they are because such knowledge would also help you identify cause-and-effect relationships in Section 3.3.3.

The more familiar you are with your economic content, the easier it is for you to recognise economic variables. When you read the extracts, ignore the specific numbers. Instead, watch out for changes (i.e., increase or decrease) in the economic variables instead. We will use Extract 1 that was first introduced in Box 3.1 as our worked example to demonstrate this. Please refer to Figure 3.2 to see how this is done.

So, for our worked example, the main point we get from the extract is that China's exports had increased. This primes your brain for macroeconomic analysis as exports is a variable in the aggregate demand

Table 3.2: Examples of economic variables.

<table>
<tr><th rowspan="2">Economic Model</th><th colspan="2">Economic Variables</th></tr>
<tr><th>Dependent</th><th>Independent</th></tr>
<tr><td>Demand and Supply</td><td>• Price
• Quantity traded</td><td>Factors affecting demand such as:
• Expectations of future price/income
• Government policy (taxes/subsidies)
• Income of consumers
• Price of related goods (substitutes/complements)
• Tastes and preferences

Factors affecting supply such as:
• Costs of production (including prices of factors of production)
• Prices of goods in joint supply/competitive supply
• Number of sellers</td></tr>
<tr><td>Aggregate Demand (AD) and Aggregate Supply (AS)</td><td>• General Price Level
• Real National Output</td><td>Components of AD and their factors such as:
• Consumption (affected by income tax rates, consumer confidence, interest rates, etc.)
• Investment (affected by corporate tax rates, business confidence, interest rates, etc.)
• Government spending (affected by the fiscal stance)
• Net exports (affected by exchange rates, foreign income levels, etc.)

Factors affecting AS such as
• Cost of production
• Quantity of factors of production in the economy
• Quality of factors of production in the economy
• Technology</td></tr>
</table>

Figure 3.2: Demonstration of ignoring numbers and focussing on economic variables.

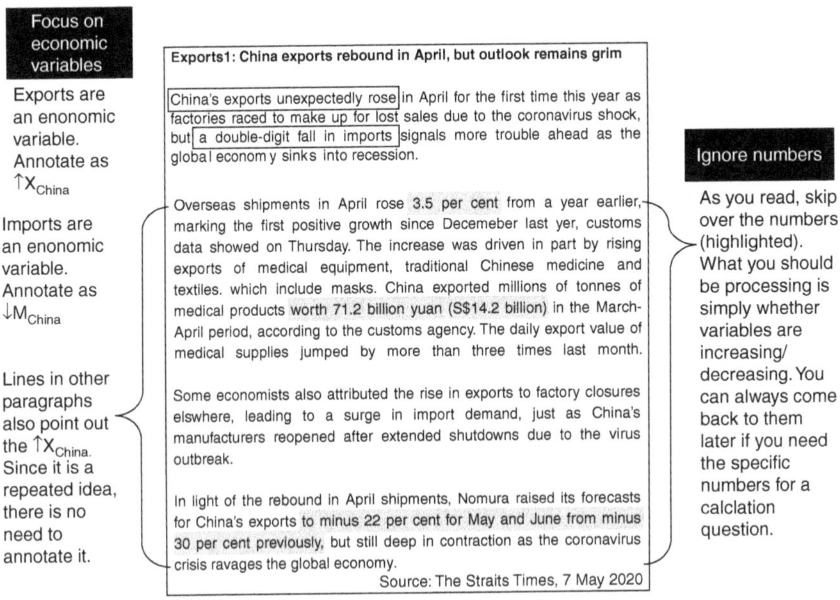

Exports1: China exports rebound in April, but outlook remains grim

China's exports unexpectedly rose in April for the first time this year as factories raced to make up for lost sales due to the coronavirus shock, but a double-digit fall in imports signals more trouble ahead as the global econom y sinks into recession.

Overseas shipments in April rose 3.5 per cent from a year earlier, marking the first positive growth since Decemeber last yer, customs data showed on Thursday. The increase was driven in part by rising exports of medical equipment, traditional Chinese medicine and textiles. which include masks. China exported millions of tonnes of medical products worth 71.2 billion yuan (S$14.2 billion) in the March-April period, according to the customs agency. The daily export value of medical supplies jumped by more than three times last month.

Some economists also attributed the rise in exports to factory closures elswhere, leading to a surge in import demand, just as China's manufacturers reopened after extended shutdowns due to the virus outbreak.

In light of the rebound in April shipments, Nomura raised its forecasts for China's exports to minus 22 per cent for May and June from minus 30 per cent previously, but still deep in contraction as the coronavirus crisis ravages the global economy.

Source: The Straits Times, 7 May 2020

and aggregate supply model. There is one mention of a reduction in imports but since the point only appeared once, it is not likely to be significant.

3.3.3 *Annotate cause-and-effect relationships*

Most extracts do not simply exist to inform you of whether economic variables are increasing or decreasing (although it is necessary to recognise that). If that were all that were required, a table or some other graphical representation would be more appropriate. Instead, extracts are included in case studies to give you qualitative information about who, what, when, where, how and why?

Paul's wheel of reasoning (or Paul's reasoning model) (Paul & Elder, 1997) is sometimes recommended as a tool to help students digest the extracts. However, while it is a good tool for developing critical thinking during reading, for A Level Economics in particular, applying the model is overkill (e.g., you will almost never need to analyse the intent of the author of the extracts). This is especially given the time constraint.

Instead, it is enough to recognise that for the A Level Economics examinations, the purpose of extracts is usually to provide cause-and-effect relationships, and/or simply to provide a list of things (e.g., a list of policy measures).

To identify the cause-and-effect relationships in an article, there are two strategies that you can use simultaneously — using English phrasing and using economic concepts.

3.3.3.1 *Identifying English phrases that illustrate cause-and-effect*

If your command of English is strong, you will naturally and unconsciously identify the cause-and-effect relationships in the extracts (in fact, if that is the case, you could skip this chapter altogether). However, if having a strong command of English is not one of your strengths, then you need to be more intentional about becoming familiar with phrasing that illustrates cause-and-effect. Table 3.3 shows a list of some common phrases that illustrate cause and effect. This list is by no means comprehensive. Still, it is a good place to start. For each sample sentence, the cause is underlined while the effect is highlighted.

3.3.3.2 *Identifying cause-and-effect using economic analysis*

The other way to identify cause-and-effect relationships is to use economic analysis. For example, from the demand and supply model, we know that income affects demand, and that demand affects price (i.e., income is an independent variable and price is a dependent variable). So, if the extract mentions a change in income and a change in price, we can fill in the gaps and deduce that the change in income is the cause and the change in price is the effect. An example from macroeconomics would be that based on the aggregate demand and aggregate supply model, we know that a change in investments

Table 3.3: Linking words to show cause and effect.

Linking Word(s)	**Sample Sentences**
Because/As	Consumers have been switching to Samsung phones *because/as* the price of iPhones has been rising.
Because of/Due to/Owing to	*Because of/Due to/Owing to* more frequent flooding, the stock of arable land has been reduced.
Since	*Since* the US has imposed tariffs on Chinese steel, the cost of producing cars in the US has increased.
So	Foreign worker levies had increased, *so* construction firms turned towards more automated processes.
Causing/Resulting in/Contributing to	Consumers developed deflationary expectations, *causing* prices to spiral downwards. Consumers developed deflationary expectations, *resulting in/contributing to* prices spiralling downwards.
Therefore/ Consequently/As a result	Oil producers ran out of storage capacity. *Therefore/ Consequently/As a result*, they were willing to sell their oil at negative prices. *As a result* of oil producers running out of storage capacity, they were willing to sell their oil at negative prices.
On the back of	Food prices rose *on the back of* biofuel subsidies diverting crops away from food production.
Attributed to	The speedy global recovery was *attributed to* the swift and coordinated response of Central Banks around the world to aggressive cut interest rates.
On account of	The unprecedentedly expansionary supplementary budget was announced *on account of* the great economic disruption caused by Covid-19.

affects aggregate demand, and that a change in aggregate demand would affect the real GDP (i.e., investments is an independent variable and real GDP is a dependent variable). So, if an extract mentions a change in investments and a change in real GDP, we can infer that the change in investments is the cause and the change in real GDP is the effect.

Note that the use of English phrasing and the use of economic analysis to identify cause-and-effect relationships are not mutually exclusive methods. They can and should be used together and/or interchangeably.

Figure 3.3: Demonstration of identifying cause-and-effect relationships.

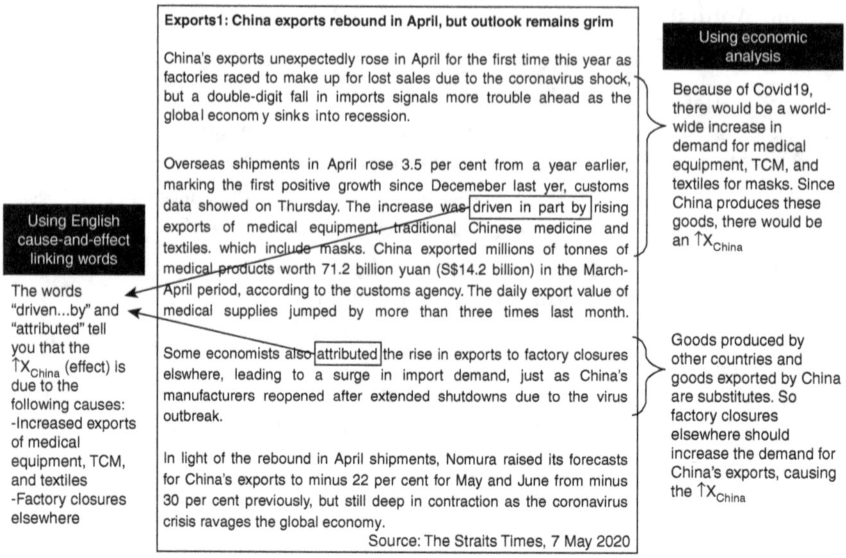

Exports1: China exports rebound in April, but outlook remains grim

China's exports unexpectedly rose in April for the first time this year as factories raced to make up for lost sales due to the coronavirus shock, but a double-digit fall in imports signals more trouble ahead as the global economy sinks into recession.

Overseas shipments in April rose 3.5 per cent from a year earlier, marking the first positive growth since Decemeber last yer, customs data showed on Thursday. The increase was driven in part by rising exports of medical equipment, traditional Chinese medicine and textiles. which include masks. China exported millions of tonnes of medical products worth 71.2 billion yuan (S$14.2 billion) in the March-April period, according to the customs agency. The daily export value of medical supplies jumped by more than three times last month.

Some economists also attributed the rise in exports to factory closures elswhere, leading to a surge in import demand, just as China's manufacturers reopened after extended shutdowns due to the virus outbreak.

In light of the rebound in April shipments, Nomura raised its forecasts for China's exports to minus 22 per cent for May and June from minus 30 per cent previously, but still deep in contraction as the coronavirus crisis ravages the global economy.

Source: The Straits Times, 7 May 2020

We now demonstrate the use of both methods to identify the cause-and-effect relationships using Extract 1 as the worked example (Figure 3.3).

So, in summary, the main points from Extract 1 are that China's exports have increased, and that this increase is due to Covid-19 increasing the demand for specific goods, as well as factory closures elsewhere causing demand to shift to China. We could annotate this in the margin using symbols (e.g., Covid-19 + Factory shutdown elsewhere → ↑X_{China}).

3.3.4 *Summarise lists*

Apart from providing cause-and-effect relationships, extracts may also be used to provide a list of things. For example, an extract could introduce a list of policy measures that a government is rolling out, a list of consequences of some factor, a list of industries that contribute most to a problem, or even a list of factors that led to some phenomenon. Note that cause-and-effect relationships and lists are not mutually exclusive. If a cause creates many effects, the many effects could

Figure 3.4: Demonstration of summarising a list.

Exports1: China exports rebound in April, but outlook remains grim

China's exports unexpectedly rose in April for the first time this year as factories raced to make up for lost sales due to the coronavirus shock, but a double-digit fall in imports signals more trouble ahead as the global economy sinks into recession.

Overseas shipments in April rose 3.5 per cent from a year earlier, marking the first positive growth since Decemeber last yer, customs data showed on Thursday. The increase was driven in part by rising exports of [1]medical equipment, [2]traditional Chinese medicine and [3]textiles. which include masks. China exported millions of tonnes of medical products worth 71.2 billion yuan (S$14.2 billion) in the March-April period, according to the customs agency. The daily export value of medical supplies jumped by more than three times last month.

Some economists also attributed the rise in exports to factory closures elswhere, leading to a surge in import demand, just as China's manufacturers reopened after extended shutdowns due to the virus outbreak.

In light of the rebound in April shipments, Nomura raised its forecasts for China's exports to minus 22 per cent for May and June from minus 30 per cent previously, but still deep in contraction as the coronavirus crisis ravages the global economy.

Source: The Straits Times, 7 May 2020

Summarising lists

The highlighted section is a list. In this case, a good summary of this list is "*industries that drove the* $\uparrow X_{China}$"

You can number each item on the list as shown on the left.

form a list. Similarly, if an effect has many causes, the many causes could form a list too.

When you recognise such lists, instead of spending too much time digesting each item on the list, you should make a note of what the list is about (i.e., summarise the list) and then simply number the items. If a question requires you to analyse one or more of the items on the list in detail, you can always do so later.

Again, we will use Extract 1 as our worked example to demonstrate this skill (Figure 3.4).

So, using all the reading skills, we know that the main point of Extract 1 is that China's exports have increased due to Covid-19 increasing the demand for specific goods, as well as factory closures elsewhere

Figure 3.5: Worked example of using reading skills to pull out main point(s) from an extract.

*The **title** tells you that the extract is about Chinese exports rising but not being expected to continue to do so.*

Extract 1: China exports rebound in April, but outlook remains grim

China's exports unexpectedly rose in April for the first time this year as factories raced to make up for lost sales due to the coronavirus shock, but a double-digit fall in imports signals more trouble ahead as the global economy sinks into recession.

Paragraph 1: *Ignoring the numbers like "double-digit", you note that economic variable here is X_{China}, which had risen unexpectedly. The word "as" tells you that this rise (the effect) was due to factories making up for lost sales. Another economic variable mentioned is M_{China} which had fallen (effect) due to the global economy sinking into a recession.*

Paragraph 2: *This paragraph explains the rise in X_{China}. Ignore all the specific numbers once you note the increase in X_{China}. The words "driven by" tells you that the increase was due to rising exports of medical equipment, traditional Chinese medicine and textiles, which include masks. You notice that these form a list (which can be summarised as specific industries whose X increased) and number them as shown. You can annotate this in the margin: Specific industries ↑X → ↑X_{china}*

Overseas shipments in April rose 3.5 per cent from a year earlier, marking the first positive growth since December last year, customs data showed on Thursday. The increase was driven in part by [1]rising exports of medical equipment, [2]traditional Chinese medicine and [3]textiles, which include masks. China exported millions of tonnes of medical products worth 71.2 billion yuan (S$14.2 billion) in the March-April period, according to the customs agency. The daily export value of medical supplies jumped by more than three times last month.

Some economists also attributed the rise in exports to factory closures elsewhere, leading to a surge in import demand, just as China's manufacturers reopened after extended shutdowns due to the virus outbreak.

Paragraph 3: *The word "attributed" tells you that another reason for the increase in X_{China} is the closure of factories elsewhere (note that this is the elaboration of the "lost sales" reason from Paragraph 1 – Chinese factories are making up for the lost sales of other factories). The economic analysis also checks out because factories elsewhere produce goods that are substitutes to Chinese exports. If they shut down, the demand for Chinese goods should increase, causing a rise in X_{China}. You can annotate this as: Factory closure elsewhere → ppl buy from China instead → ↑D for X_{china} → ↑X_{china}*

In light of the rebound in April shipments, Nomura raised its forecasts for China's exports to minus 22 per cent for May and June from minus 30 per cent previously, but still deep in contraction as the coronavirus crisis ravages the global economy.

Paragraph 4: *"In light of" tells you that because of the ↑X_{china}, Nomura (a rating agency) raised its forecast for China's exports (notice again that we ignore the specific numbers of -22% and -30%). Also the word "as" in the later part of the sentence tells us that China's exports are expected to stay low due to the coronavirus crisis. You can annotate as: Corona crisis → ↓D for X_{china}*

Source: The Straits Times, 7 May 2020

causing demand to shift to China. We also know that there is a list of what the specific goods are, but we will only analyse them in detail if the question demands it.

Note that because the worked example uses a fairly short extract, there is only one main point. If the extracts are longer, there could be a few main points.

It is also good to reiterate that because a book must be written (and hence, also read) in a sequential manner, it appears that the reading skills that have been explained are meant to be carried out step-by-step. However, that is far from the truth. Apart from having to read the extract's title first, the other three skills of ignoring numbers and focussing on economic variables, annotating cause-and-effect relationships, and summarising lists are meant to be done simultaneously when you read the extract itself. This is demonstrated as we read through our worked example from top to bottom (Figure 3.5).

So, the key points of this extract are that (1) Chinese exports had risen because specific industries' exports had risen as factories producing these goods in other countries had shut down (shutdown of other factories $\rightarrow \uparrow D$ for X_{China}), and (2) this rise is not expected to continue due to the Coronavirus crisis depressing global demand (Covid-19 $\rightarrow$ global recession $\rightarrow \uparrow D$ for X_{China}). We can probably ignore the bit on the fall in X_{China} since it is just a small part of the article.

References

Bransford, J.D. & Johnson, M.K. (1972). Contextual prerequisites for understanding: Some investigations of comprehension and recall. *Journal of Verbal Learning and Verbal Behaviour*, 717–726.

Paul, R. & Elder, L. (1997, April). *The elements of reasoning and the intellectual standards.* Retrieved from The Foundation for Critical Thinking website: https://www.criticalthinking.org/pages/the-elements-of-reasoning-and-the-intellectual-standards/480

Chapter 4

Understanding the Case Material — Interpreting Numerical/Graphical Data

4.1 Introduction

In every case study question, there will be 2–3 pages of case study material before the questions. The case material will include both textual and numerical data (including graphs). Since the questions are based on the case study, it is important to understand the case material. Additionally, this must be accomplished within a short span of no more than 10 minutes per question to leave you with enough time to complete your answers. This chapter shows you the skills required to understand the numerical data (including graphs) in the shortest amount of time.

First, you will need to identify which economic variable is being presented (refer to Section 3.3.2 in Chapter 3 to recall what economic variables are) and what type of data it is being presented as. The type of numerical data provided in case studies usually fall into one of the following categories:

- Raw data
- Indices (singular form "Index")
- Percentage change data

- Proportions
- Ratios[1]
- Balances

To identify the economic variable and the data type, observe the title of the figure and the units of the values. Generally, the title should tell you which economic variable is being presented and the units should tell you what type of data it is presented as. Note that the units are sometimes provided within the title too. Table 4.1 shows some examples of titles and units for the different types of data.

Then, for each type of data, you need to be able to interpret what the changes in the figures mean in terms of whether the variable has increased or decreased and by how much it has done so.

Table 4.1: Examples of titles and units for different data types.

Sample Titles	Sample Units[a]	Type of Data
• Price of maize • GDP of USA	• USD • USD	Raw data
• Consumer price index • Formula milk price index	None	Indices Indices have no units. They always have a base year/month though.
• GDP growth rate • Year-on-year change in consumption expenditure • Percentage change in mobile phone usage	%	Percentage change data All percentage changes are expressed in %
• Market share of top four smartphone companies • Government expenditure as share of GDP • Unemployment rate of US	%	Proportions Proportions are usually expressed in %
• GDP per capita • Labour productivity	• USD/head • Output/worker	Ratios

(Continued)

Table 4.1: (*Continued*)

Sample Titles	Sample Units[a]	Type of Data
• China's balance of trade (BOT) with US • Singapore government budget balance	• USD • % of GDP	Balances The units of a balance would depend on whether the balance is expressed as absolute data (in which case, it would be expressed in a currency such as USD) or a proportion (in which case it would be expressed as a %)

Note: [a]Technically, % is not a unit as it just denotes a proportion out of a base of 100 (e.g., 70% just means 0.7). This is in contrast to kg or USD which are actual units. Nonetheless, I will use the term "units" loosely to include %.

4.2 Interpreting Raw Data

Raw data is unmanipulated data. It is best understood in contrast to indices and percentage change data that will be explained in the subsequent sections. An example of raw data is provided Figure 4.1.

Note that the same data could also be presented in a graph or chart such as those presented in Figure 4.2.

Regardless of whether it is presented as a table of values (as in Figure 4.1) or a line graph/bar chart (as in Figure 4.2), what we need to do remains the same — determine the economic variable and the type of data we are looking at by reading the title and the units.

4.2.1 *How to recognise raw data*

First, from reading the title, we know that the economic variable that we are looking at is the price of maize (or corn. Maize is the American term). Then, we pay attention to the units. Figure 4.1 shows an example where the unit "USD per metric tonne" is in the title. This unit tells us that the data we are looking at is raw data since it is unmanipulated (i.e., not expressed as an index or a percentage change, etc.). Sometimes, the units may not be in the title. They could be in the figure instead. For example, in Figure 4.2, both the line graph and bar

Figure 4.1: Example of raw data.

Price of Maize (USD per metric tonne), Oct-2019–Apr-2020

Month	Maize (USD per metric tonne)
Oct-19	167.15
Nov-19	166.33
Dec-19	166.96
Jan-20	171.79
Feb-20	168.71
Mar-20	162.42
Apr-20	146.91

Source: indexmundi.com. Retrieved on 17 May 2020 from: https://www.indexmundi.com/commodities/?commodity=corn

Figure 4.2: Example of raw data presented using a line graph and bar chart.

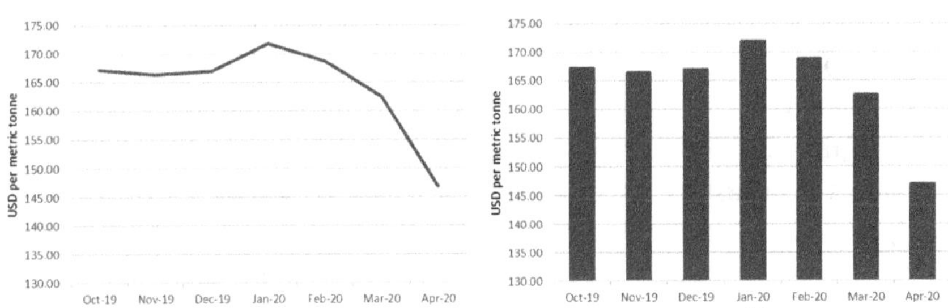

(a) (b)

Source: indexmundi.com.

chart showed the units "USD per metric tonne" in the labelling of the vertical axis. Regardless of where the unit is situated, once we have found it and ascertained that the data is raw data, we can move on.

4.2.2 *How to interpret raw data*

Raw data is the easiest form of data to interpret. With this data, we know exactly what the value of the variable is and can easily see whether and how much it has increased in both absolute and percentage terms (absolute is in contrast to percentage, as the next example will show). For example, using the set of data in Figure 4.1, we know that maize was priced at \$167.15 per metric tonne (a tonne is 1000 kg) in October 2019 and that the price fell to \$146.91 by April 2020. The overall fall (or the extent of the fall) was \$20.24 in absolute terms (\$167.15 – \$146.91) and 12.11% in percentage terms ((\$167.15 – \$146.91)/\$167.15 × 100%). We can also see the monthly variation in the price in between.

4.3 Interpreting Indices

In contrast to raw data, indices have been through some manipulation. Indices are constructed from raw data. A base year (or month, or even day) of the raw data is chosen and then all other data points are expressed as a percentage of the base year data. We illustrate this by converting our raw data from Figure 4.1 into an index.

Let us imagine that we use October 2019 as the base month. Then, all the data points would be expressed as a percentage of the Maize price in October 2019 (Figure 4.3).

You should notice two things about index data — that the value at the base year must be exactly 100 and that the % sign is usually just dropped. Note that in this example, the index was created based on setting the base month's value as 100. However, the base value could have been set as 1 instead. In that case, instead of having a value of 99.51 for Nov-19, we would have a value of 0.9951; instead of having a value of 99.89 for Dec-19, we would have a value of 0.9989, and instead of having a value of 102.78 for Jan-20, we would have a

Figure 4.3: Converting raw data into an index.

Month	Maize (USD per metric tonne)
Oct-19	167.15
Nov-19	166.33
Dec-19	166.96
Jan-20	171.79
Feb-20	168.71
Mar-20	162.42
Apr-20	146.91

Express each month's price as a % of the base month's price (i.e, \$167.15, which is the price in the base month of Oct-19)

Month	Maize Price Index (Base month = Oct-19)
Oct-19	100 (167.15/167.15 x 100)
Nov-19	99.51 (166.33/167.15 x 100)
Dec-19	99.89 (166.96/167.15 x 100)
Jan-20	102.78 (171.79/167.15 x 100)
Feb-20	100.93 (168.71/167.15 x 100)
Mar-20	97.17 (162.42/167.15 x 100)
Apr-20	87.89 (146.91/167.15 x 100)

value of 1.0278, etc. Note also that the base month need not be the first month in the data set. It could have been an earlier month (and therefore not shown in the data set) or a later month.

4.3.1 *How to recognise indices*

To determine whether the data you come across in the case study material is index data, you should look out for two things. First, look out for the term "index" or "indices" in the title. That will tell you that the data is an index. Second, look out for a base year/month (base years are more typical than base months). If there is a base year/month, then the data is an index (even if the title did not state that it is an index). For example, in Figure 4.4, even though the title just states "Maize Prices", the fact that the vertical axis states that "Base month = Oct-2019" tells you that the data provided is an index.

4.3.2 *How to interpret indices*

If you are provided with index data, then you can only interpret whether the values have increased or decreased (i.e., an increase in the price index of maize must mean that the price of maize has increased). You can also calculate the extent of the change in percentage terms by calculating the percentage change in the price index (e.g., if the price

Figure 4.4: Maize prices, Oct-2019–Apr-2020.

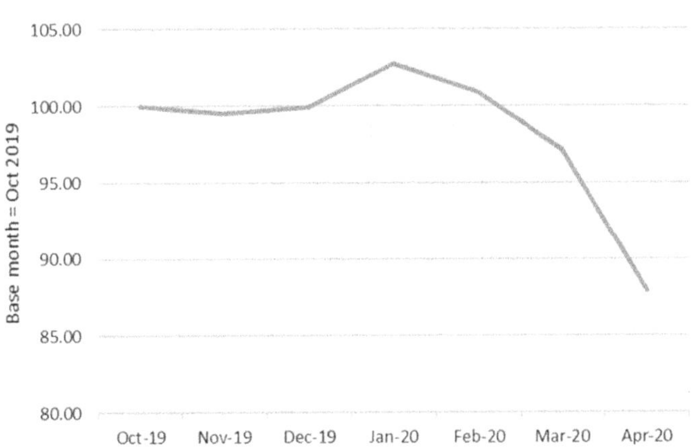

index of maize increases by 5% (e.g., from 50 to 52.5), the price of maize must also have increased by 5%). However, with a price index, you can neither infer what the actual price is (i.e., you cannot tell if maize is $100 per tonne or $50 per tonne or any other amount) nor the change in the actual price in absolute terms (i.e., you cannot tell if the maize price had increased by $5 or $10 or any other amount). This would have implications on data comparison questions, which will be explained in Chapter 5.

4.4 Interpreting Percentage Change Data

Percentage change data is, as its name suggests, data that shows percentage changes. It is the type of data that students most frequently misinterpret.

To understand percentage change data, let us first see how it is constructed from raw data. The percentage change in a variable's value is calculated using the following familiar formula.[2] We use this formula to convert the raw data from Figure 4.1 to percentage change data (Figure 4.5).

$$\%\Delta = \frac{\text{Value}_{\text{New}} - \text{Value}_{\text{Old}}}{\text{Value}_{\text{Old}}} \times 100\%.$$

Figure 4.5: Converting raw data to percentage change data.

Month	Maize (USD per metric tonne)
Oct-19	167.15
Nov-19	166.33
Dec-19	166.96
Jan-20	171.79
Feb-20	168.71
Mar-20	162.42
Apr-20	146.91

Express each month's price as a % Δ from the previous month's price using the formula:

$$\%\Delta = \frac{Value_{New} - Value_{Old}}{Value_{Old}} \times 100\%$$

Month	Percentage Change in Maize Prices (%)
Oct-19	Nil (no previous month data)
Nov-19	$-0.49\% = \frac{166.33 - 167.15}{167.15} \times 100\%$
Dec-19	$0.38\% = \frac{166.96 - 166.33}{166.33} \times 100\%$
Jan-20	$2.89\% = \frac{171.79 - 166.96}{166.96} \times 100\%$
Feb-20	$-1.79\% = \frac{168.71 - 171.79}{171.79} \times 100\%$
Mar-20	$-3.73\% = \frac{162.42 - 168.71}{168.71} \times 100\%$
Apr-20	$-9.55\% = \frac{146.91 - 162.42}{162.42} \times 100\%$

You should notice a few things about the percentage change data — the unit is "%" and the values could be positive or negative. A negative percentage change corresponds to a decrease in the value (e.g., from Oct-19 to Nov-19, the price of maize decreased from US$167.15 to US$166.33 per metric tonne and the percentage change was –0.49%) whereas a positive percentage change corresponds to an increase in the value (e.g., from Nov-19 to Dec-19, the price of maize increased from US$166.33 to US$166.96 per metric tonne to and the percentage change was 0.38%). You should also notice that the larger the change, the larger the value of the percentage change (ignoring the sign). For example, the decrease in the price of maize from Jan-20 to Feb-20 was US$3.08 per metric tonne and shows up as a percentage change of –1.79%. The decrease from Feb-20 to Mar-20 was larger at US$6.29 per metric tonne and had a larger number for the percentage change of –3.73% (ignoring the sign).

4.4.1 *How to recognise percentage change data*

To determine whether the data you come across in the case study material is percentage change data, you should look out for two things in the title and the unit. First, look out for the term "change" or "growth rate" or some synonym in the title. That is a hint that the data is percentage change data. Second, look out to see if the unit is in %. If the title is "change in (some variable)" and the unit is in "%", then the data is percentage change data. For example, in Figure 4.6, even though the title just states "Change in Maize Prices Compared to Previous Month", the fact that the unit on the vertical axis is "%" tells you that the data provided is percentage change data.

Note that you must not immediately think that the data is percentage change data simply because the unit is "%". There must also be evidence from the title that the data presented is some sort of change. This is because proportions (the next section) also use "%" as the unit.

Figure 4.6: Change in maize prices compared to previous month, Nov-2019–Apr-2020.

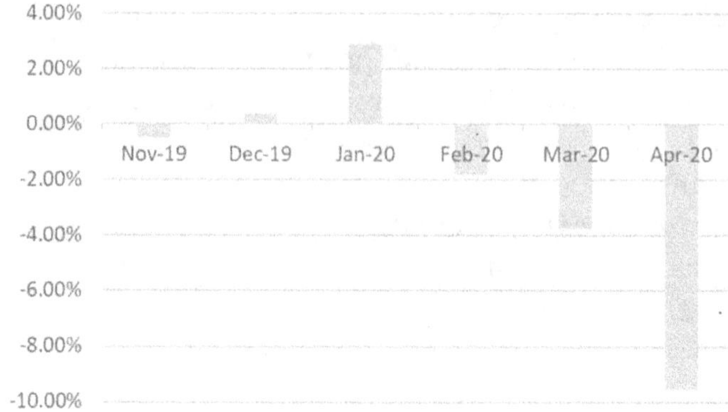

4.4.2 *Interpreting percentage change data*

If you are provided with percentage change data, then you can interpret whether the values have increased or decreased (by looking at the percentage changes were positive or negative), how much it has done so (by looking at the values and ignoring the sign), and the rate of change (e.g., whether it was increasing at an increasing rate or increasing at a decreasing rate). For example, looking at Figure 4.6, you can tell that the price of maize decreased from Oct-19 to Nov-19 (negative %Δ for Nov-19), then increased from Nov-19 to Jan-20 (positive %Δ for both Dec-19 and Jan-20), then decreased again (negative %Δ for remaining months). Since the negative %Δs outweigh the positive %Δs over the entire period (a rule-of-thumb you can apply is to simply sum up all the percentage changes to see if you have a positive or negative number overall), you can infer that prices must have fallen overall. Additionally, you can also see a pattern in the last three data points where the %Δs were becoming more negative each month. This implies that the price was falling by a larger and larger extent. As such, you can also deduce that the price was decreasing at an increasing rate in the last few months.

However, with just percentage change data, you cannot tell what the actual price is. This would have implications on data comparison questions, which will be explained in Chapter 5.

4.5 Interpreting Proportions/Ratios

Proportion data refers to when some data is represented as a percentage/proportion of some other data. A ratio is just how many times the value of one variable is of another's. The two will be explained together because they have similarities.

To understand proportions, let us first see how proportion data is constructed from raw data. To do so, we use a common macroeconomic indicator that is proportion data — the unemployment rate. The unemployment rate is calculated using the following familiar formula. We will use this formula to convert the raw data on the number of unemployed people and the size of the labour force in Singapore into Singapore's unemployment rate (Figure 4.7).

$$\text{Unemployment rate}\,(\%) = \frac{\text{Number of unemployed people}}{\text{Number of people in the labour force}} \times 100\%.$$

You should notice that the unit for proportion data (the unemployment rate in this case) is "%", which is the same as the unit for percentage change data. This is why we cannot determine whether the data in the case study is percentage change or proportion data just

Figure 4.7: Converting raw data to proportion data (unemployment rate).

Year	Labour force (thousands)	Employed (thousands)	Unemployed (thousands)
2018	3675.6	3575.3	100.3
2019	3740.8	3630.0	110.8

Express each year's unemployment as the unemployment rate using the formula:

$$UnE\ (\%) = \frac{No.of\ UnE}{No.of\ ppl\ in\ LF} \times 100\%$$

Year	Unemployment rate (%)
2018	$2.73\% = \frac{100.3}{3675.6} \times 100\%$
2019	$2.96\% = \frac{110.8}{3740.8} \times 100\%$

Source: Labour force and Employment data extracted from singstat.gov.sg. Retrieved on 17 May 2020 from: https://www.singstat.gov.sg/find-data/search-by-theme/economy/labour-employment-wages-and-productivity/latest-data

based on observing "%" as the unit since both types of data have the same unit.

Ratios are like proportions in that they are both just fractions. In fact, proportions are just a subset of ratios. For example, 50% (proportion) is the same as 1/2 (fraction), which is the same as 1:2 (ratio). The only thing to note is that in A Level Economics, ratios are seldom expressed as (whole number):(whole number). Instead, the base (the number on the right) is always normalised to 1. So, 1:2 would be expressed as 0.5:1 and hence just written as 0.5. Similarly, 5:4 would be expressed as 1.25:1 and hence just written as 1.25.

4.5.1 *How to recognise proportion/ratio data*

4.5.1.1 *For proportions*

To determine whether the data you come across in the case study material is proportion data, you should look out for two things in the title and the unit. First, look out for the term "as share of" or "as a proportion of" or "% of (some variable) in (some other variable)" or some synonym in the title. That is a hint that the data is proportion data. Second, look out to see if the unit is %. For example, if the title is "Share of FDI in an economy's total investments" or "consumption as share of GDP" and the unit is in "%", then the data is proportion data.

Having said that, there are some common indicators that you must know are proportion data even though it may not be stated in the title. One is the unemployment rate (which we used as an illustration in Figure 4.7) and the other is the market share of firms (or the *n*-firm concentration ratio). Components of GDP are also often, but not always, presented as proportions of GDP for comparisons across countries.

4.5.1.2 *For ratios*

Ratios would usually have the word "per" in the title. For example, "GDP per capita" is the ratio of the GDP to the size of the population, which gives you the average GDP per person. However, there are also variables that may not have the word "per" in the title even though they are ratios. One such example is labour productivity. Labour productivity is the output per worker. As such, it is a ratio. However, the case material may only label the data as "labour productivity" or just "productivity". Units-wise, ratios would have the units such as USD/person, output/worker, etc.

4.5.2 *Interpreting proportion/ratio data*

Because a proportion is basically a fraction (i.e., 50% is the same as 1/2 or 2/4 or 3/6, etc.), the interpretation of proportion data is complicated. This is because an increase in a proportion (e.g., 50% to 60%) could be the result of the numerator (the top number in a fraction) increasing and the denominator (the bottom number in a fraction) remaining constant (e.g., 5/10 to 6/10), or the numerator increasing and the denominator decreasing (e.g., 8/16 to 9/15), or the numerator increasing and the denominator also increasing but by a smaller extent (e.g., 7/14 to 9/15), or the numerator remaining constant and the denominator decreasing (e.g., 9/18 to 9/15), or the numerator decreasing and the denominator also decreasing but by a larger extent (e.g., 10/20 to 9/15). If you convert each of the fractions in the previous sentence into a percentage, you will see that they all translate into 50% increasing to 60% although the reasons for the increase are clearly very different.

Since ratios are also fractions (i.e., 1:2 is the same as 1/2 or 2/4 or 3/6, etc.), the paragraph before this also applies to ratios — an increase/decrease in a ratio could have many interpretations.

The full range of interpretations of a change in proportion or ratio data is presented in Table 4.2.

From Table 4.2, what you can see is that when you see a change in proportion or a change in a ratio, you cannot be sure whether the

Table 4.2: Interpretations of a change in proportion or ratio data.

Change in Proportion or Ratio	Possible Interpretations
Proportion or ratio increases (e.g., an increase in the unemployment rate, an increase in GDP per capita)	• Numerator increasing and the denominator remaining constant (e.g., no. of unemployed increasing while size of labour force remains constant, GDP increasing while size of population remains constant) • Numerator increasing and the denominator decreasing (e.g., no. of unemployed increasing while size of labour force decreases, GDP increasing while size of population decreases) • Numerator increasing and the denominator also increasing but by a smaller extent[a] (e.g., no. of unemployed increasing by 10% while size of labour force increases by 5%, GDP increasing by 10% while size of population increases by 5%) • Numerator remaining constant and the denominator decreasing (e.g., no. of unemployed remaining constant while size of labour force decreases, GDP remaining constant while size of population decreases) • Numerator decreasing and the denominator also decreasing but by a larger extent (e.g., no. of unemployed decreasing by 5% while size of labour force decreases by 10%, GDP decreasing by 5% while size of population decreases by 10%)
Proportion or ratio remaining constant (e.g., unemployment rate is constant, GDP per capita is constant)	• Numerator and the denominator both increasing by the same extent (e.g., no. of unemployed and size of labour force both increasing by 10%, GDP and size of population both increasing by 10%) • Numerator and the denominator both remaining constant (e.g., no. of unemployed and size of labour force both not changing, GDP and size of population both not changing) • Numerator and the denominator both decreasing by the same extent (e.g., no. of unemployed and size of labour force both decreasing by 10%, GDP and size of population both decreasing by 10%)
Proportion or ratio decreases (e.g., a decrease in the unemployment rate, a decrease in the GDP per capita)	• Numerator decreasing and the denominator remaining constant (e.g., no. of unemployed decreasing while size of labour force remains constant, GDP decreasing while size of population remains constant) • Numerator decreasing and the denominator increasing (e.g., no. of unemployed decreasing while size of labour force increases, GDP decreasing while size of population increases)

Table 4.2: (*Continued*)

Change in Proportion or Ratio	Possible Interpretations
	• Numerator decreasing and the denominator also decreasing but by a smaller extent (e.g., no. of unemployed decreasing by 10% while size of labour force decreases by 5%, GDP decreasing by 10% while size of population decreases by 5%) • Numerator remaining constant and the denominator increasing (e.g., no. of unemployed remaining constant while size of labour force increases, GDP remaining constant while size of population increases) • Numerator increasing and the denominator also increasing but by a larger extent (e.g., no. of unemployed increasing by 5% while size of labour force increases by 10%, GDP increasing by 5% while size of population increases by 10%)

Note: [a]This happens to be the case for the example given in Figure 4.7. However, you would not have known this if you had only been given the change in the unemployment rate and nothing else.

numerator or denominator had increased or decreased or stayed constant.

Having said that, in the context of A Level Economics, the proportion data provided is usually of the type where the denominator does not change very much. For example, for unemployment rate, the denominator is the number of people in the labour force. Since the number of people in the labour force mainly only changes due to retirement or deaths (which reduce the size of the labour force) and entry of school-leavers (e.g., fresh graduates from tertiary of secondary education institutions) into the labour force (which increases the size of the labour force), we should expect the size of the labour force to not change very much from year to year as retirement/death rates and graduation rates tend to change slowly. The implication of this is that since the denominator is not expected to swing by much, changes in the proportion data will likely reflect changes in the numerator. Returning to the unemployment rate example, since the labour force can be assumed to stay almost constant on a year-to-year basis, an increase/decrease in the unemployment rate can be interpreted as an increase/decrease in the number of unemployed people. So, in summary, for proportion data that appears in A Level Economics examinations, you can usually interpret the change in the proportion as the change in the numerator. So, an increase/decrease in the proportion means an increase/decrease in the numerator and the larger/smaller the change in the proportion, the larger/smaller the change in the numerator. However, when you do so, you should also bear in mind that this just one interpretation amongst others (in case this particular interpretation does not make sense when viewed together with other information).

For ratios, however, without further information, you will not be able to tell how the numerator and denominator have changed. For example, if there is an increase in labour productivity, it could be because more output has been produced by the same number of workers, or the same amount of output is being produced but by fewer workers. Without further information, you cannot tell which case it is. However, if at least the change in the numerator or denominator is provided, then you can infer the change in the other. For example, if you are given the information that GDP per capita had increased by 5% and that the population had increased by 2%, then you can infer that the GDP must have increased by greater than 5% (estimated to be 7% in this case).

4.6 Interpreting Balances

Balances refer to data where some sort of monetary outflow is subtracted from a monetary inflow.

For example, the balance of trade (BOT) is a balance where monetary outflow from a country in the form of import expenditure (M) is subtracted from monetary inflow into a country in the form of export revenue (X) (i.e., BOT = $X - M$). Another example would be the government budget balance where monetary outflow from a government's coffers in the form of government expenditure (G) is subtracted from monetary inflow into a government's coffers in the form of tax revenue (T) (i.e., governmnet budget balance = $T - G$). A final less obvious balance encountered in A Level Economics is the profit

Figure 4.8: Converting raw data to a balance (BOT).

Year	US export revenue (billion USD)	US import expenditure (billion USD)
2016	115.6	462.4
2017	129.8	505.2
2018	120.1	539.7
2019	106.6	452.2

Convert into balance of trade using the formula: BOT = X − M

Year	US balance of trade (billion USD)
2016	-346.8 = 115.6 − 462.4
2017	-375.4 = 129.8 − 505.2
2018	-419.5 = 120.1 − 539.7
2019	-345.6 = 106.6 − 452.2

Source: United States Census Bureau. Retrieved on 17 May 2020 from: https://www.census.gov/foreign-trade/balance/c5700.html

earned by a firm. In this case, monetary outflow from a firm in the form of incurring costs of production (COP or total cost (TC)) is subtracted from monetary inflow collected by a firm in the form of total revenue (TR) (i.e., Profits = TR – TC). Let us look at how a balance is computed from raw data using the US BOT in goods with China as an example (Figure 4.8).

You should notice that the unit for the balance follows the unit of the data from which it was computed. For example, in Figure 4.8, the BOT is in billion USD because the export revenue and import expenditure were both in billion USD. If export revenue and import expenditure had both been given as a proportion/percentage of GDP, then the BOT would also be presented as a proportion/percentage of GDP.

You should also notice that balances can have either positive or negative values (although Figure 4.8's example only had negative values).

4.6.1 *How to recognise a balance*

To determine whether the data you come across in the case study material is a balance, you should read the title. The title should contain the word "balance" (e.g., BOT, budget balance) or "net"/"nett" (e.g., net/nett factor income from abroad). The unit will not be helpful as a balance could be presented in both absolute terms (like what was shown in Figure 4.8) or as a proportion (e.g., BOT as a % of GDP).

Having said that, there is one type of economic data that you must know is a balance even though its name/title no hint at all. That data is the profit earned by a firm (Profits = TR – TC). This is rarely tested though.

4.6.2 *Interpreting a balance*

There are two parts to interpreting a balance. The first is whether the inflow of money exceeds the outflow of money. If a balance has a positive value, the monetary inflow exceeds the outflow. This is usually called a "surplus". Conversely, if a balance has a negative value, the monetary outflow exceeds the inflow. This is usually called a "deficit". If the monetary inflow equalled the monetary outflow, then the balance would be zero. We say that the balance is "balanced". For example, using the data from Figure 4.8, we see that the US BOT in goods with China was consistently negative from 2016 to 2019. This means that in each of those years, the import expenditure (the monetary outflow) exceeded the export revenue (the monetary inflow). In other words, the US BOT in goods with China was consistently in a deficit.

The other part to interpret is the change in the balance. The balance could improve (become more positive/less negative) or worsen (become more negative/less positive). Any change in a balance could have a few possible interpretations which are summarised in Table 4.3.

Table 4.3: Interpretations of a change in a balance.

Change in Balance Data	Possible Interpretations
Balance improved (e.g., BOT became more positive or less negative)	• Monetary inflow increased and monetary outflow remained constant (e.g., export revenue increased while import expenditure remained constant) • Monetary inflow increased and monetary outflow decreased (e.g., export revenue increased while import expenditure decreased)

Table 4.3: (*Continued*)

Change in Balance Data	Possible Interpretations
	• Monetary inflow and outflow both increased but to a smaller extent for outflow (e.g., export revenue increased by US$10 billion and import expenditure increased by US$5 billion) • Monetary inflow remained constant and monetary outflow decreased (e.g., export revenue remained constant while import expenditure decreased) • Monetary inflow and outflow both decreased but to a larger extent for outflow (e.g., export revenue decreased by US$5 billion and import expenditure decreased by US$10 billion)
Balance remaining constant (e.g., no change in the BOT)	• Monetary inflow and outflow both increased by the same extent (e.g., export revenue and import expenditure both increased by US$10 billion) • Monetary inflow and outflow both remained unchanged (e.g., export revenue and import expenditure both stayed constant) • Monetary inflow and outflow both decreased by the same extent (e.g., export revenue and import expenditure both decreased by US$10 billion)
Balance worsened (e.g., BOT became more negative or less positive)	• Monetary inflow decreased and monetary outflow remained constant (e.g., export revenue decreased while import expenditure remained constant) • Monetary inflow decreased and monetary outflow increased (e.g., export revenue decreased while import expenditure increased) • Monetary inflow and outflow both decreased but to a smaller extent for inflow (e.g., export revenue decreased by US$10 billion and import expenditure decreased by US$5 billion) • Monetary inflow remained constant and monetary outflow increased (e.g., export revenue remained constant while import expenditure increased) • Monetary inflow and outflow both increased but to a larger extent for outflow (e.g., export revenue increased by US$5 billion and import expenditure increased by US$10 billion)

From Table 4.3, what you can see is that like proportion data, when you see a change in a balance, you cannot be sure whether the monetary inflow or outflow had increased or decreased. As such, you would need information from other sources such as the extracts or other tables/figures to determine whether the monetary inflow and outflow had increased/decreased.

4.7 Interpreting Elasticities (A Special Case)

Elasticity values deserve its own section because these values are a combination of percentage change and ratios.

4.7.1 *Price elasticity of demand*

Let us examine the formula for one of the elasticities — price elasticity of demand (PED) — to see how this is so:

$$\text{PED} = \frac{\%\Delta \text{ in Quantity demanded of a good} \left(Q_D\right)}{\%\Delta \text{ in Price of the good} \left(P\right)}.$$

The numerator and denominator are both percentage change data, and the fraction shows that we are looking at the ratio of the %Δ in Q_D to the %Δ in P.

We can apply our understanding of percentage change data and ratios to interpret the PED value.

First, if the PED is negative, it must mean that either %Δ in Q_D is negative and %Δ in P is positive, or %Δ in Q_D is positive and %Δ in P is negative. For the former scenario, since we know that a negative %Δ means a decrease and a positive %Δ means an increase, the first scenario means that Q_D falls and P rises. Using the same logic, the latter scenario means that Q_D rises and P falls. So, a negative PED value means that Q_D and P have an inverse relationship since when one rises, the other falls.

Figure 4.9: Interpreting PED values.

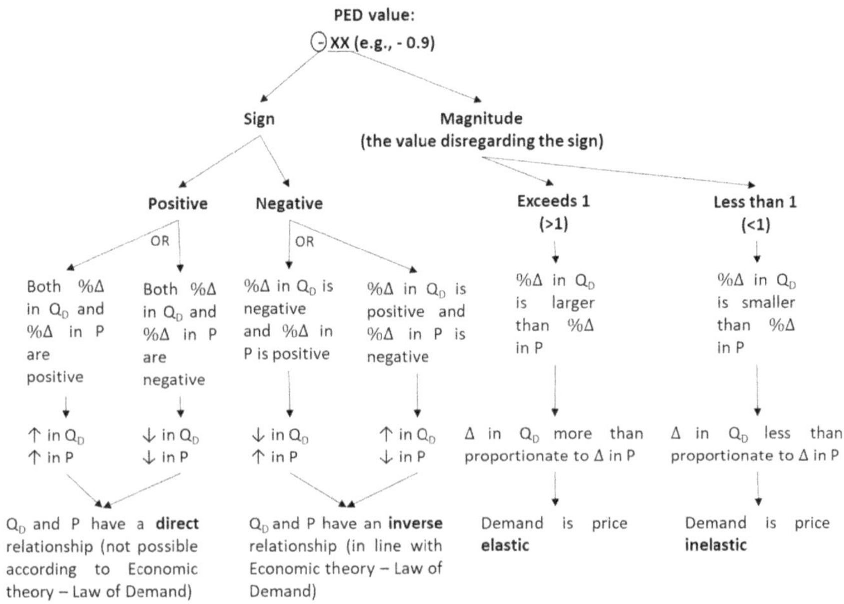

Next, disregarding the sign of the PED value, if the value is more than 1, it would mean that the numerator (%Δ in Q_D) exceeds the denominator (%Δ in P). This would mean that the Q_D is changing more than proportionately in response to a change in price. Conversely, if the value is less than 1, it would mean that the numerator (%Δ in Q_D) is smaller than the denominator (%Δ in P). This would mean that the Q_D is changing less than proportionately in response to a change in price.

The above is summarised in Figure 4.9.

So, a PED value of –0.9 (in Figure 4.9) means that the demand of the good is price inelastic, where a 1% increase in the price would cause a 0.9% decrease in its quantity demanded.

We can then summarise all the values of PED on a number line and include the special cases of perfectly price elastic, perfectly price inelastic, and unitary price elastic demand. Note that these special cases are rarely tested on account of them being so specific (Figure 4.10).

Figure 4.10: PED values on a number line.

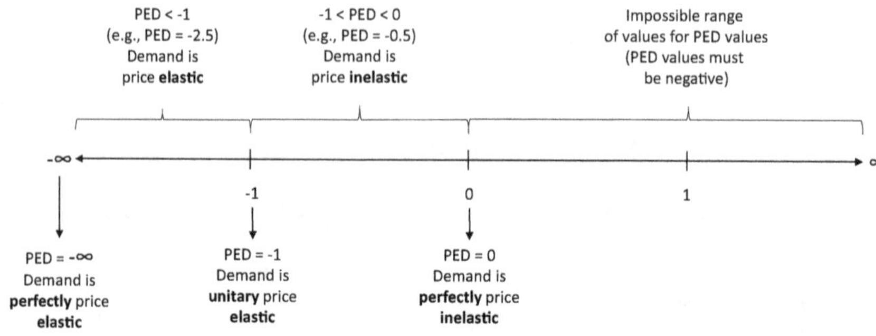

The same line of thinking in terms of considering the significance of the sign and the magnitude can be applied to the other elasticity concepts to figure out how to interpret their values too.

4.7.2 *Price elasticity of supply*

The formula for price elasticity of supply (PES) is

$$\text{PES} = \frac{\%\Delta \text{in Quantity supplied of a good} \left(Q_S\right)}{\%\Delta \text{in Price of the good} \left(P\right)}.$$

Based on this formula, a summary of how to think about the significance of the sign and magnitude of PES is presented in Figure 4.11.

So, a PES value of 0.9 (in Figure 4.11) means that the supply of the good is price inelastic, where a 1% increase in the price would cause a 0.9% increase in its quantity supplied.

Like what we did with PED, we can then summarise all the values of PES on a number line and include the special cases of perfectly price elastic, perfectly price inelastic, and unitary price elastic supply. Note that these special cases are rarely tested on account of them being so specific (Figure 4.12).

Figure 4.11: Interpreting PES values.

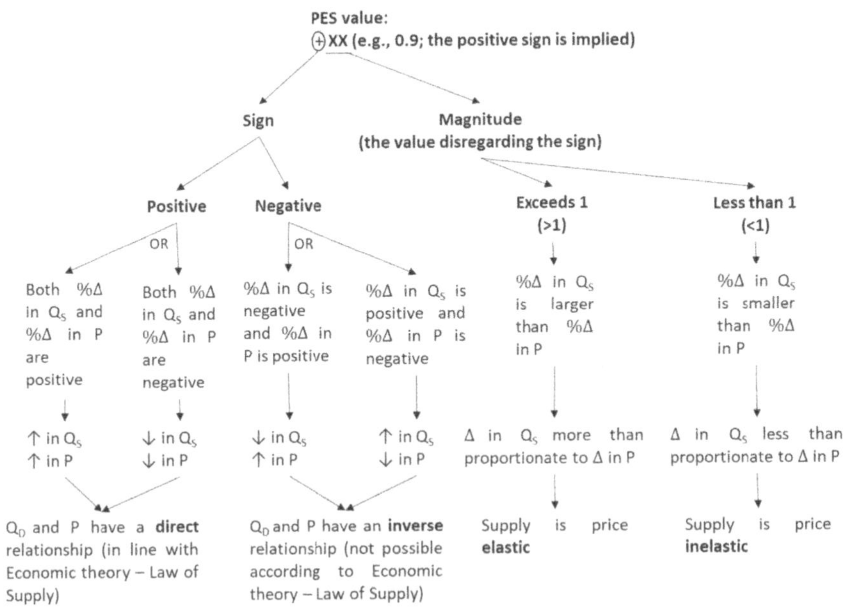

Figure 4.12: PES values on a number line.

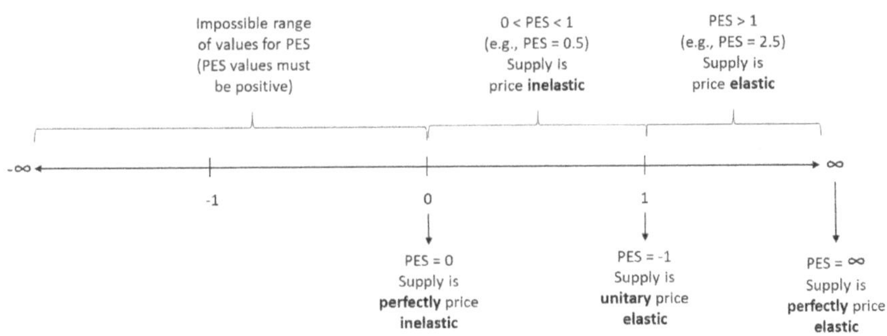

4.7.3 *Income elasticity of demand [not in H1 Economics 8843 syllabus]*

The formula for income elasticity of demand (YED) is

$$\text{YED} = \frac{\%\Delta \text{in Quantity demanded of a good} (Q_D)}{\%\Delta \text{ in Income} (Y)}.$$

Figure 4.13: Interpreting YED values.

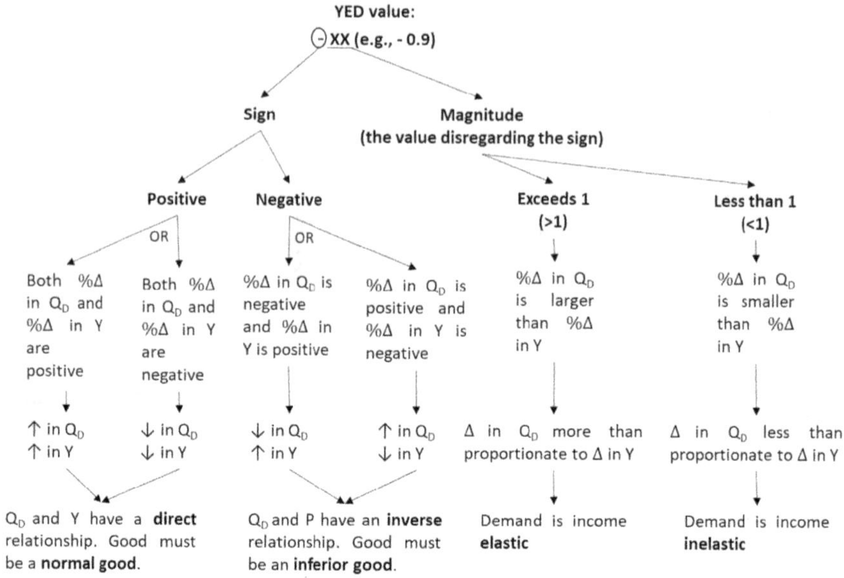

Based on the formula for the value of YED, a summary of how to think about the significance of the sign and magnitude of YED is presented in Figure 4.13.

So, a YED value of –0.9 (in Figure 4.13) means that the demand of the good is income inelastic, and that a 1% increase in the income would cause a 0.9% decrease in its quantity demanded. The good is an inferior good.

Like what we did with the previous elasticities, we can then summarise all the values of YED on a number line and include the special cases of perfectly income elastic, perfectly income inelastic, and unitary income elastic demand. Note that these special cases are unlikely to ever be tested on account of them being so specific (Figure 4.14).

Note also that for normal goods (YED > 0), we further divide them into two categories. Normal goods with income inelastic demands (YED < 1) are called necessities while normal goods with income elastic demands (YED > 1) are called luxury goods.

Figure 4.14: YED values on a number line.

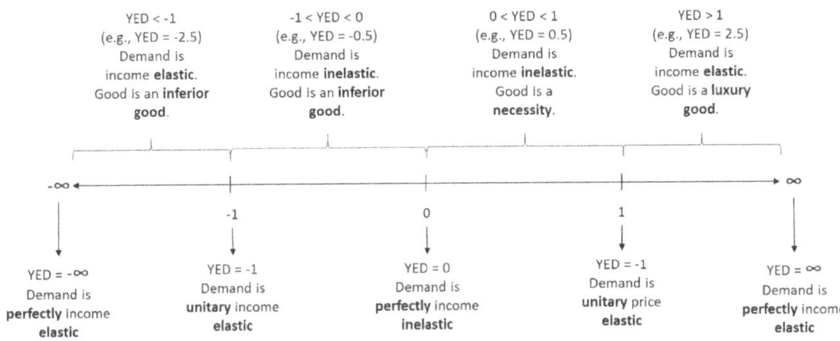

4.7.4 *Cross elasticity of demand [not in H1 Economics 8843 syllabus]*

The formula for cross elasticity of demand (XED) is

$$\text{XED} = \frac{\%\Delta \text{in Quantity demanded of a good } A\left(Q_{DA}\right)}{\%\Delta \text{in price of another good } B\left(P_B\right)}.$$

Based on this formula, a summary of how to think about the significance of the sign and magnitude of XED is presented in Figure 4.15.

So, an XED value of –0.9 (in Figure 4.15) means that the demand of good A is cross inelastic to the price of good *B*, and that a 1% increase in the price of good B would cause a 0.9% decrease in good *A*'s quantity demanded. Goods *A* and *B* are weak complements.

Like what we did with the previous elasticities, we can then summarise all the values of XED on a number line and include the special cases of perfectly cross elastic, perfectly cross inelastic, and unitary XED. Note that these special cases are unlikely to ever be tested on account of them being so specific (Figure 4.16).

Figure 4.15: Interpreting XED values.

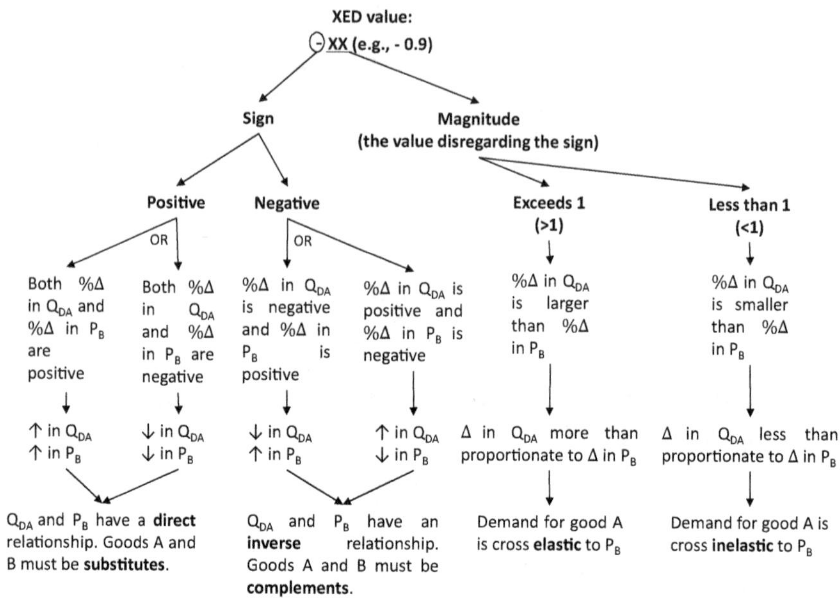

Figure 4.16: XED values on a number line.

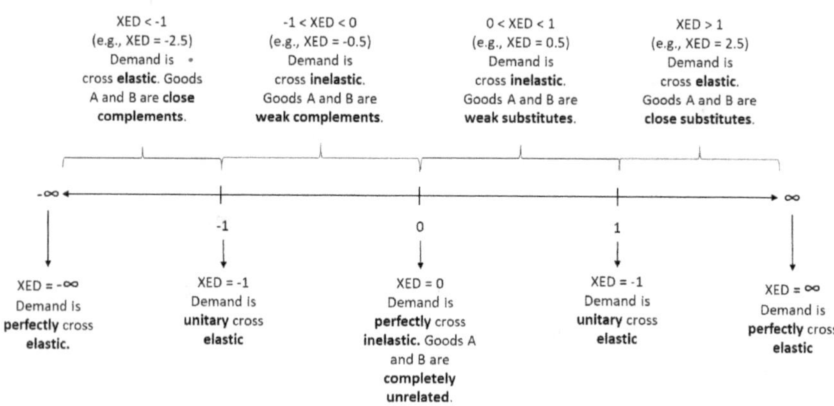

4.7.5 *Summary of skills to understand the case study material*

Use the case study question's title to determine the question's focus (micro/macro).

For each extract

1. Read the extract's title to anchor your brain;
2. Ignore numbers and focus on economic variables;
3. Annotate cause-and-effect relationships;
4. Summarise lists.

For each table/figure

Use the title of the table/graph and the units to identify the economic variable and data type:

- Raw data (title should state what it is; units will likely be $ or USD or kg, etc.);
- Indices (title should state "index" and a base year/base month is specified);
- Percentage change data (title should indicate it is some sort of change over time; unit is %);
- Proportions (title should it indicate that it is the share of something; unit is %);
- Ratio (title should include the word "per"; unit should be (variable)/(variable));
- Balances (title should state "balance").

Interpret the values

- Raw data (straightforward to read);
- Indices (straightforward to read if it has increased/decreased; cannot tell actual value);
- Percentage change data (positive %Δ means an increase and negative %Δ means a decrease; rising magnitude (e.g., 5% to 10% or –5% to –10%) means that the increase/decrease is at an

increasing rate and falling magnitude (e.g., 10% to 5% or –10% to –5%) means that the increase/decrease is at a decreasing rate);

- Proportions (increase/decrease in the proportion usually (but not always) can be interpreted as an increase/decrease in the numerator of the proportion);
- Ratios (increase/decrease in the ratio could mean numerator/denominator increased/decreased. Not possible to interpret without further data);
- Balances (positive values mean that monetary inflow exceeds outflow and negative values mean that monetary outflow exceeds inflow).

For interpreting elasticity values

Split the value into two parts — the sign and the magnitude (i.e., the value disregarding the sign). Interpret each part separately.

- Use the sign (positive/negative) to determine whether the numerator and denominator in the formula have a direct (positive sign) or inverse (negative sign) relationship;
- Use the magnitude to determine whether the demand/supply is elastic (magnitude > 1 means that the demand/supply is elastic and magnitude < 1 means that the demand/supply is inelastic).

Endnotes

1. Indices are actually ratios too. However, it has its own section because of its uniqueness to Economics.
2. Δ is the short form for "change".

Chapter 5
Answering the Case Study Questions

5.1 Introduction

In this section, we study the skills to answering the part-questions (i.e., questions (a), (b), (c), etc. in each case study). Recall that 1(a), 1(b), etc. are considered part-questions because the entire case study is considered one question. However, for ease of writing (and reading), let us use the term "question" to replace "part-questions" from this point onwards. Before writing your answer to the questions, you should analyse them to find out their requirements so that you can write an answer that meets the requirements. Each question has three components — the question number, the question phrasing, and the marks carried. Each component should be analysed. How to do so is summarised in Figure 5.1.

Of the three components, the analysis of the question phrasing is the most important. This explains why the term "question analysis" usually refers to the analysis of the question phrasing even though the question number and mark allocation also provide useful information. Nonetheless, we will go through the analysis of each part in order from left to right (question number, question phrasing, and mark allocation).

Figure 5.1: Components of a question and what to do for each component.

(a) With reference to Extract 1, explain why "Chinese exports...rose". [4]

This is the question number. Use it to determine whether are other sub-parts that are relevant to this question.

This is the question phrasing. Use the 3C+ framework (command, content, context + additional condition(s)) to analyse it

This is the mark allocation. Use it to determine how much to write and whether to "zoom in" or "zoom out"

5.1.1 *Analysing the question number*

The question number tells you whether the question is related to an earlier question. Sub-parts (e.g., (ai) and (aii)) are always related in some way. For example, question (aii) could be related to (ai) in the sense that the answer to (ai) has some implications on the answer for (aii). For example, (ai) may require a calculation of the PED and that value of PED is supposed to be applied to analyse a change in total revenue in (aii). This is illustrated in Figure 5.2.

In this example, when answering (aii), the demand for crude oil should be taken to be price elastic/inelastic based on the calculation in (ai).

Alternatively, sub-parts could also be related in that some direction is given in a question that has to be applied to all the sub-parts. For example, (a) may state "Using Extract 1". If so, both the answers to (ai) and (aii) must be based on Extract 1. This is illustrated in Figure 5.3.

Figure 5.2: Example of sub-parts being related due to one sub-part's answer affecting another's.

(a) (i) With reference to Extract 1, calculate the price elasticity of demand (PED) for crude oil. [2]

(ii) Explain how an increase in the price of crude oil would affect the total revenue of crude oil producers like OPEC. [3]

Figure 5.3: Example of sub-parts being related due to sub-parts having to take the same direction.

(a) Using Extract 1:

(i) Calculate the price elasticity of demand (PED) for crude oil. [2]

(ii) Explain why crude oil producers like OPEC cut oil production. [3]

In this example, both the answers for (ai) and (aii) must be based on Extract 1.

Note that while (ai) and (aii) are considered sub-parts and should therefore be related, (a) and (b) are not considered sub-parts (they are separate questions) and are usually unrelated.

5.1.2 *Analysing the question phrasing — The 3C+ framework*

To analyse the question phrasing, use the 3C+ framework. The three "C"s refer to the command word, content, and context. You need to identify each "C" in the question to determine what the question requires. The "+" refers to additional conditions such as which extract or figure you are supposed to refer to. You should identify them in sequence (i.e., identify the command word first, then the content words, then the context words (if any), and finally the additional conditions (if any).

5.1.2.1 *What is a command word?*

The command word is the word that tells you what to do (i.e., the verb[1]). For example, "Describe" is the command word in the question phrase: "Describe the trend in the price of vegetables from 2010 to 2019". Other examples of command words include "compare", "calculate", "explain", "discuss", etc.

Table 5.1: Examples of command words in sample question phrases.

Command Word	Sample Question Phrase
Describe	Using Table 1, **describe** the trend in the price of vegetables from 2010 to 2019.
Compare	With reference to Figure 2, **compare** the GDP growth rates of Zimbabwe and Ethiopia.
Calculate	Referring to Extract 3, **calculate** the price elasticity of supply (PES) of Norwegian salmon.
State	**State** a factor that determines the extent to which the increase in the value-added tax (VAT) would increase the price of a good.
Identify	**Identify** the policy stance that the Monetary Authority of Singapore (MAS) adopted in Extract 4.
Suggest	**Suggest** a reason for the "poor outlook on global trade" (Extract 5).
Infer	**Infer** the change in Australia's GDP from the information provided in Table 6.
Define	**Define** the term "positive externalities".
Explain	Using the information from Figure 7, **explain** why coffee prices are on the increase.
Discuss	In view of the problems faced by each of the economies described in Extract 8, **discuss** whether expansionary policies will be effective in helping these governments achieve their macroeconomic objectives.

It is important to identify the command word because each type of command word has its own requirements. Table 5.1 shows a list of the commonly used command words and how they may appear in questions.

You should notice that the command word is not necessarily the first word of the question phrase. There could be other instructions such as "Using Table 1" or "With reference to Figure 2" that precede the command word. To identify the command word, look for the word that commands you to do something. It is the word that takes the form as if it were following the word "to" (i.e., "to describe").

The specific requirements of each command word are explained in the later sections of this chapter. For example, the requirements of a "describe" question is in the section titled "How to answer a "Describe" (or a synonym) question".

5.1.2.2 *What does content refer to?*

After you have identified the command word, you need to identify the content that you are supposed to apply the command word to. Let us use a non-examination example to illustrate this. Supposed you were given a command to "kick". The content would be what is to be kicked. So, if you were told to "kick the ball", the command word would be "kick" and the content would be "the ball".

The same applies to examination questions. If you were asked to "Describe the trend in the price of vegetables from 2010 to 2019", the command word would be "describe" and the content to be described would be "the trend in the price of vegetables from 2010 to 2019".

An easy way to identify the content after identifying the command word is to add the word "what" after the command word to make it sound like a question. The answer to that question would be the content. For example, for the question "Describe the trend in the price of vegetables from 2010 to 2019", the command word is "Describe". So, you could have the following conversation with yourself (but not out loud of course. You should not be speaking during an examination. And, even if you were not in an examination hall and are just doing some practice questions, you do not want to be perceived as an oddball.)

You ask: "Describe what?"

You answer: "The trend in the price"

The answer to the "(Insert command word) what?" question is the content.

Table 5.2: Examples of command and content words in sample question phrases.

Sample Question Phrase
Using Table 1, **describe** the trend in the price of vegetables from 2010 to 2019.
With reference to Figure 2, **compare** the GDP growth rates of Zimbabwe and Ethiopia.
Referring to Extract 3, **calculate** the price elasticity of supply (PES) of Norwegian salmon.
State a factor that determines the extent to which the increase in the value-added tax (VAT) would increase the price of a good.
Identify the policy stance that the Monetary Authority of Singapore (MAS) adopted in Extract 4.
Suggest a reason for the "poor outlook on global trade" (Extract 5).
Infer the change in Australia's GDP from the information provided in Table 6.
Define the term "positive externalities".
Using the information from Figure 7, **explain** why coffee prices are on the increase.
In view of the problems faced by each of the economies described in Extract 8, **discuss** whether expansionary policies will be effective in helping these governments achieve their macroeconomic objectives.

We return to our sample question phrases in Table 5.1 to provide more examples of the content of the questions. This is illustrated in Table 5.2 where the command words remain in **bold** type and the content words are highlighted.

You might notice that the content words seem to be the words that immediately follow the command word. That would be true almost all the time. However, as the saying goes, for every rule, an exception (or exceptions, really). The question phrase "Better to have government failure than market failure. Discuss." is an exception to the rule. The command word is "Discuss" and the content to be discussed is whether it is "(b)etter to have government failure than market failure". In this case, the content words came before the command word. Nonetheless, such phrasing is less common.

The content words determine what is relevant to the question (e.g., which economic models are relevant). The specifics of how to tell what is relevant will be covered in the later sections of this chapter when we look at worked examples in the sections titled "How to answer a... question".

5.1.2.3 *What does context refer to?*

Context refers to the situational information. This could be the specific market/economy being analysed, the period of analysis (e.g., 2018 vs 2019), or any other information regarding where, when, who, etc.

Examples of the context of the sample questions we have looked at thus far are provided in Table 5.3. In this table, the command words remain in **bold** type, the content words are highlighted, and the context words are *italicised.*

You should notice a few things. First, most of the time, the context refers to a market(s) (if the question is on microeconomics) or an economy(s) (if the question is on macroeconomics). Second, not all

Table 5.3: Examples of command, content, and context words in sample question phrases.

Sample Question Phrase	Context
Using Table 1, **describe** the trend in the price of *vegetables* from *2010 to 2019.*	The market is the vegetable market and the years are 2010 to 2019.
With reference to Figure 2, **compare** the GDP growth rates of *Zimbabwe* and *Ethiopia.*	The economies in the question are Zimbabwe and Ethiopia.
Referring to Extract 3, **calculate** the price elasticity of supply (PES) of *Norwegian salmon.*	The market is the Norwegian salmon market.
State a factor that determines the extent to which the increase in the value-added tax (VAT) would increase the price of a good.	This question has no context. It is a theory question.
Identify the policy stance that the *Monetary Authority of Singapore (MAS)* adopted in Extract 4.	The economy in the question is the Singapore economy (MAS is Singapore's central bank).
Suggest a reason for the "poor outlook on *global* trade" (Extract 5).	The economy in the question is the global economy.

(*Continued*)

Table 5.3: (*Continued*)

Sample Question Phrase	Context
Infer the change in *Australia's* GDP from the information provided in Table 6.	The economy in the question is Australia.
Define the term "positive externalities".	This question has no context. It is a theory question.
Using the information from Figure 7, **explain** why *coffee* prices are on the increase.	The market is the coffee market.
In view of the problems faced by *each of the economies* described in Extract 8, **discuss** whether expansionary policies will be effective in helping these governments achieve their macroeconomic objectives.	The economies in the question are those mentioned in Extract 7.

questions will have a context. There were two questions within the sample questions without a context. Having said that, in a case study, the norm is for most, if not all, question to have a context.

5.1.2.4 *What are additional conditions?*

Additional conditions refer to things like "Using Table 1" or "With reference to Extract 2".

Table 5.4 shows more examples of additional conditions using the sample questions we have looked at thus far. In this table, the command words remain in **bold** type, the content words are highlighted, the context words are *italicised*, and the additional conditions are underlined.

You should notice a few things about additional conditions. They usually (but not always) direct you to the relevant case study material. An example of an exception would be "Using aggregate demand and aggregate supply analysis, explain how a recovery in the US could stoke inflation in Brazil". In this example, the additional condition does not direct you to relevant case study material. Instead, it tells you which economic model you should use. You should also notice that not all questions have additional conditions.

Table 5.4: Examples of command, content, context words and additional conditions.

Sample Question Phrase
Using Table 1, **describe** the trend in the price of *vegetables* from *2010 to 2019.*
With reference to Figure 2, **compare** the GDP growth rates of *Zimbabwe* and *Ethiopia.*
Referring to Extract 3, **calculate** the price elasticity of supply (PES) of *Norwegian salmon.*
State a factor that determines the extent to which the increase in the value-added tax (VAT) would increase the price of a good. *This question does not have additional conditions.
Identify the policy stance that the *Monetary Authority of Singapore (MAS)* adopted in Extract 4.
Suggest a reason for the "poor outlook on *global* trade" (Extract 5). *This question does not have additional conditions. The "(Extract 5)" just tells you that the quote "poor outlook on global trade" came from Extract 5. The suggested reason need not be from there.
Infer the change in *Australia's* GDP from the information provided in Table 6.
Define the term "positive externalities". *This question does not have additional conditions.
Using the information from Figure 7, **explain** why *coffee* prices are on the increase.
In view of the problems faced *by each of the economies* described in Extract 8, **discuss** whether expansionary policies will be effective in helping these governments achieve their macroeconomic objectives.

Usually, just based on the three "C"s, what the question requires should already be clear. The additional conditions are usually included to narrow the students' search for relevant information or for the relevant economic model/concept. For example, if we just apply the three "C"s to the question "Using Extract 2, calculate the price elasticity of demand (PED) for maize", it would be apparent that what we need to do is to apply the PED formula to maize and compute its value. The additional condition of "Using Extract 2" simply saves you time by directing you to the extract which has the relevant information for us to calculate the PED of maize.

An unfortunate side-effect of additional conditions narrowing the search for relevant information/economic models/concepts is that the range of acceptable answers also naturally becomes smaller since the answers must be based on the table/figure/extract specified or use the economic model/concept specified.

5.1.3 *Summary of the 3C+ framework*

3C+

The three "C"s are:
- Command word
- Content
- Context

"+" refers to additional condition(s)

In summary, the 3C+ framework refers to the identification of the:

- First "C" — Command word
    - This word tells you what to do (e.g., describe, compare, explain)
    - Every question must have at least one. Most questions have only one but it is possible for a question to have more
- Second "C" — Content
    - This tells you what the command word is applied to
    - Can be identified by answering the question "(insert command word) what?"
    - Every command word must be applied to a piece of content
- Third "C" — Context
    - This usually tells you which market(s) to look at (for microeconomics) or which economy(s) to look at (for macroeconomics)
    - It could also tell you which time period to focus on
    - Most case study questions have this, but not always
- "+" — Additional condition(s)
    - This generally tells you which case material to refer to or which economic model/concept to apply
    - Some case study questions will have this

You should identify the three "C"s before the "+" because the three "C"s would be enough to tell you what the question requires. The "+" just makes your life easier by directing you to the relevant case material or economic model/concept to use in your answer.

Finally, note that while the command word and the additional conditions are usually clear, the line between which words are part of content and which are part of the context is not a distinct one. The good news is that you do not need to be precise in terms of exactly which words are the content words and which are the context words. This is because even if you classify them slightly differently, you would still be able to identify the correct question requirement. For example, for the question "Describe the trend in the price of vegetables from 2010 to 2019", you could identify the content as "the trend in the price" and the context as "vegetables" and "from 2010 to 2019". Alternatively, you could identify "the trend in the price of vegetables from 2010 to 2019" as the content, with "vegetables" and "from 2010 to 2019" as context words embedded within the content. Both ways (and other variants) are equally correct.

5.1.4 *Analysing the mark allocation*

The mark allocation tells you how much you need to write, and whether you need to "zoom in" or "zoom out". The relationship between the marks allocated and how much you need to write, as well as the concepts of "zooming in" and "zooming out" will be explained in the later sections titled "How to answer a... question".

We will see how all the different elements of question analysis (i.e., taking note of the question number, applying the 3C+ framework, and taking note of the mark allocation) help you to find out the question requirements by working through the different types of questions.

5.2 How to Answer a "Describe" (or a Synonym) Question

A "describe" question is a question with the command word "describe" or a synonym of "describe". For example, the question "Describe the trend in the price of Robusta Coffee from Oct-19 to Apr-20" is a "describe" question as the command word is "Describe".

Table 5.5: Command words which are synonymous with "describe".

Command Word/Phrase	Sample Question
Describe...	Describe the trend in the price of Robusta Coffee from Oct-19 to Apr-20 shown in Figure 1.
Summarise...	Summarise the trend in the price of Robusta Coffee from Oct-19 to Apr-20 shown in Figure 1.
State what happened to...	State what happened to the price of Robusta Coffee from Oct-19 to Apr-20 shown in Figure 1.

The question "Summarise the trend in the price of Robusta Coffee from Oct-19 to Apr-20" is also a "describe" question because the command word "Summarise" is a synonym of "describe".

Examples of command words which tell you that the question is a "describe" question are presented in Table 5.5.

Although the command words are different, all three questions are asking for the exact same thing.

The content and context (in this case, "the trend in the price of Robusta Coffee from Oct-19 to Apr-20") tell you what you should be describing and the additional condition, if provided, (in this case, "as shown in Figure 1") tells you where to find it. Note that while most "describe" questions require you to describe trends, it may not always be the case. The content to be described could be a relationship instead (e.g., "Describe the relationship between the price of Robusta Coffee and the price of Arabica coffee from Oct-19 to Apr-20 shown in Figure 1").

If the time period of observation (in this case "from Oct-19 to Apr-20") is not provided, then describe the entire range of data provided in the figure/table. Also, note that the figure/table might provide you with irrelevant data (e.g., provide you with the prices of two goods when the question only requires you to describe the trend in the price of one good). In such a scenario, be careful to not read the wrong set of data.

5.2.1 *Mark allocation*

"Describe" questions are marked by points and how the marks are allocated depends on whether a trend or a relationship is to be described, and if it is a trend, what type of data is being described (refer to Chapter 4 to see the different types of data).

5.2.1.1 *For describing trends*

If the data to be described is a balance (e.g., balance of trade), the first mark is awarded for stating whether the balance is in surplus or deficit. The second mark is then awarded for providing the general trend. Subsequently, one mark is awarded for each refinement provided. This means that for a question that asks you to describe a balance, if only 1 mark is allocated, the question only requires you to state whether the balance is in surplus or deficit. If 2 marks are allocated, then the question requires the statement of surplus/deficit and the general trend. If 3 marks are allocated, then the question requires the statement of surplus/deficit, the general trend, and another refinement. If 4 marks are allocated, then the question requires the statement of surplus/deficit, the general trend, and two refinements. The last few scenarios are unlikely as it is seldom that "describe" questions carry more than 2 marks.

If the data to be described is not a balance (e.g., the price of a good), then it is not possible to have a statement of surplus/deficit. So, the first mark would be awarded for providing the general trend and subsequently, one mark is awarded for each refinement provided. This means that if only 1 mark is allocated, the question only requires you to provide the general trend. If 2 marks are allocated, then the question requires the general trend and one refinement. If 3 marks are allocated, then the question requires the general trend and two refinements. This last scenario is unlikely as it is seldom that "describe" questions carry more than 2 marks.

5.2.1.2 *For describing relationships*

For a description of a relationship, the first mark is allocated to the general relationship in terms of whether it was a direct or inverse one

Table 5.6: Mark allocation for "describe" questions.

Describe...	
...a trend	**...a relationship**
First mark: (Only applicable if the data is a balance) Statement of surplus/deficit Next mark: General trend Next mark: First refinement Next mark: Second refinement . . Where to stop depends on how many marks are allocated	First mark: General relationship Next mark: First refinement Next mark: Second refinement . . . . . Where to stop depends on how many marks are allocated

(also known as "positive" or "negative" relationships). Each subsequent mark is provided for a refinement to the relationship. This means that if only 1 mark is allocated, the question only requires you to provide the general relationship. If 2 marks are allocated, then the question requires the general relationship and one refinement. Descriptions of relationships seldom carry more than 2 marks.

We summarise the mark allocation for "describe" questions in Table 5.6.

5.2.2 *How to answer it — Description of a trend*

5.2.2.1 *(For balances only) Writing the statement of surplus/deficit*

The statement of surplus/deficit is straightforward. If the balance is positive (e.g., balance of trade = \$5 billion), then it is in surplus. If the balance is negative (e.g., balance of trade = –\$5 billion), then it is in deficit. The terminology only changes for profits. If the profit is positive (e.g., profit = \$1 million), then we say that the firm is making profit (or supernormal profit). If the profit is negative (e.g., profit = –\$1 million), then we say that the firm is making losses (or subnormal profit). However, a description of profits is very unlikely to be tested.

5.2.2.2 *Writing the general trend*

The general trend refers to whether the value has increased or decreased overall. The proper way to do so is to draw (or imagine) a best fit line for all the data points and see if the line slopes upwards (increase) or downwards (decrease). In fact, there are statistical techniques to do so (e.g., regression). However, that would clearly be overkill for the A Levels. For the A Levels, the general trend can be seen from simply comparing the first and last points to see if there has been an increase/decrease.

Note that if the data is a balance, then we use the terms "improved/worsened" to describe the balance position instead of "increased/decreased". "Increased/Decreased" can be used, however, to describe the surplus/deficit (not the balance position). A surplus increasing means that the balance has become more positive and a deficit increasing means that the balance has become more negative. Table 5.7 summarises what phrasing is acceptable for describing the general trend of a balance.

You can refer to Chapter 4 to see how to interpret different types of data (e.g., percentage change data) to see if the value of the variable has increased/decreased.

Table 5.7: Summary of acceptable phrasing for describing the general trend of a balance.

Phrasing	Acceptable/Not Acceptable
The balance position (or just "balance") improved/worsened	Acceptable
The balance position (or just "balance") increased/decreased	Not acceptable
The surplus increased/decreased	Acceptable
The deficit increased/decreased	Acceptable

5.2.2.3 *Writing the refinement*

Many students think that quoting the exact figures constitute a refinement. That is wrong. Quoting numbers adds no value to the answer at all. Instead, refinements refer to features of the data that stand out, apart from the general trend. Specifically, you should look out for:

- Exceptions
- Sharpest change in the same direction as the general trend
- Rate of change

- **Exceptions** — Exceptions would be the years when the data moved opposite to the general trend. For example, if the price of Robusta Coffee generally decreased from Oct-19 to Apr-2019, then an increase from Oct-19 to Nov-2019 would be an exception. This is illustrated in Figure 5.4.

If there are multiple periods of exceptions, either write down the largest exception or state all the periods of exceptions.

- **Sharpest change in the same direction as the general trend** — The sharpest change in the same direction as the general trend

Figure 5.4: Robusta Coffee (USD per kg).

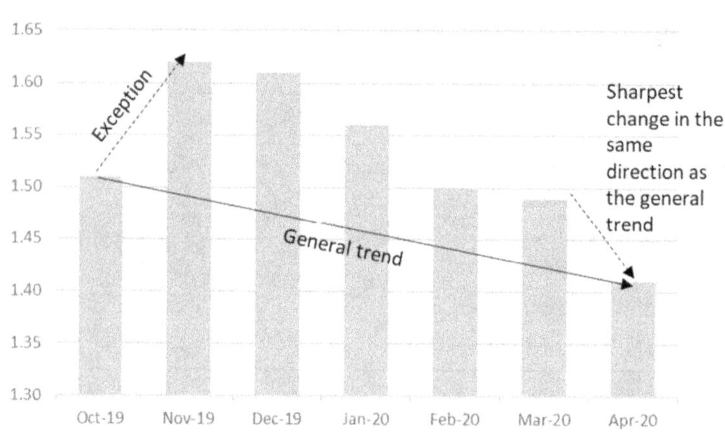

Source: indexmundi.com. Retrieved on 17 May 2020 from: https://www.indexmundi.com/commodities/?commodity=robusta-coffee

refers to when the data changed the most while still in the same direction as the general trend. It is significant because it tells you which period contributed the most to the general trend. For example, in Figure 5.5, the price of Robusta Coffee geneally decreased from Oct-19 to Apr-2020. And, the largest decrease was observed from Mar-2020 to Apr-20.

If you cannot be sure which is the largest change in the same direction as the general trend, then state all the periods when you observed these large changes.

- **Rate of change** — The rate of change refers to whether the data is changing at an increasing rate (i.e., the changes are getting larger and larger) or at a decreasing rate (i.e., the changes are getting smaller and smaller). You would need more data points to ascertain this and it is possible that the data has no clear rate of change.

Table 5.8 provides some examples of how to interpret the rate of change.

Note that we would also not use rate of change as a refinement if we can see that there is a clear rate of change but only for a small section of the data. For example, in the last figure in Table 5.8, the price of Arabica coffee seemed to be increasing at a decreasing rate from

Table 5.8: Interpreting the rate of change.

<table>
<tr><th>Data</th><th>Interpretation</th></tr>
<tr><td>Table: Change in maize price from previous month

<table><tr><th>Month</th><th>%</th></tr><tr><td>Feb-20</td><td>–1.79</td></tr><tr><td>Mar-20</td><td>–3.73</td></tr><tr><td>Apr-20</td><td>–9.55</td></tr></table>
Source: indexmundi.com. Retrieved on 17 May 2020 from: https://www.indexmundi.com/commodities/?commodity=corn</td><td>The fall in price is becoming bigger over time (fell by 1.79% from Jan to Feb, then by 3.73% from Feb to Mar, and finally by 9.55% from Mar to Apr).

So, we say that the maize prices are decreasing at an **increasing rate**.</td></tr>
</table>

(*Continued*)

Table 5.8: (*Continued*)

Data	Interpretation
Figure: Rice (USD per metric tonne) 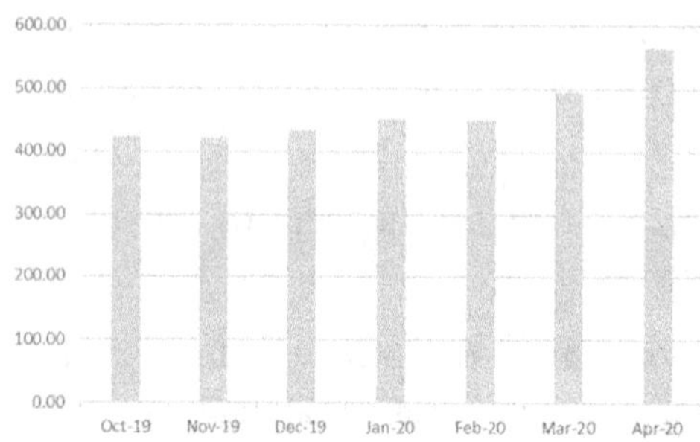 *Source*: indexmundi.com. Retrieved on 17 May 2020 from: https://www.indexmundi.com/commodities/?commodity=rice.	We do not have the exact numbers but visually, apart from the exception from Jan to Feb, the price of rice seems to be increasing by only small amounts in the earlier months and then by larger and larger amounts in the later months. So, we say that the price of rice is increasing at an **increasing rate.**
Figure: Price of Arabica Coffee (USD per kg) 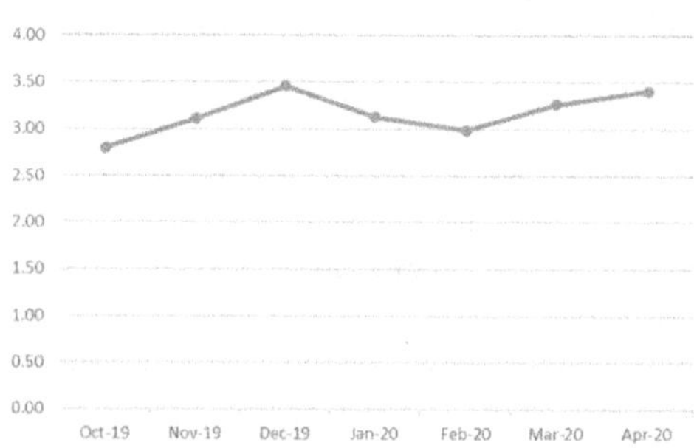 *Source*: indexmundi.com. Retrieved on 17 May 2020 from: https://www.indexmundi.com/commodities/?commodity=other-mild-arabicas-coffele	There is no clear rate of change in this data. So, we would not use rate of change as a refinement.

Feb-20 to Apr-20 as the increase from Mar-20 to Apr-20 was smaller than the increase from Feb-20 to Mar-20. However, the data spans 7 months. So, we do not use rate of change as a refinement since we only saw a clear rate of change for 3 of the 7 months.

Once you can identify all the possible refinements (i.e., exceptions, sharpest change in the same direction as the general trend, rate of change), then it is a matter of selecting which refinement to write in your answer. Always select the most salient (or most obvious) refinement. Exceptions are usually the most obvious but that is not always the case. For example, if the data has a general decreasing trend with an exception where there was a minuscule and almost undetectable increase and a period where there is an extremely sharp decrease, then the extremely sharp decrease should be the refinement that you highlight.

5.2.3 *How to answer it — Description of a relationship*

5.2.3.1 *Writing the general relationship*

The general relationship is either a direct or inverse one. A direct relationship between two variables is when the two variables increase and/or decrease together. An inverse relationship is observed when one variable changes in the opposite direction as the other. For example, when one goes up, the other comes down.

The proper way to determine the relation between variables should be to calculate a statistical measure called the correlation coefficient, which, if positive, shows a direct relationship and, if negative, shows an inverse relationship. However, for the A Level examination, an eyeball test should be enough. If the two variables seem to be moving in sync, then they have a direct relationship. If they move in opposite directions, they have an inverse relationship. This is illustrated in Figure 5.5.

With reference to Figure 5.5, Series A and Series B seem to be moving together generally. So, they have a generally direct relationship. Series A and Series C, however, consistently go in the opposite direction. So, they have a generally inverse relationship.

If the relationship is not very clear, you can look at the general trend of each variable and make your judgement from there. If the general trend for both variables are the same (i.e., both generally increased/

Figure 5.5: Direct and inverse relationships.

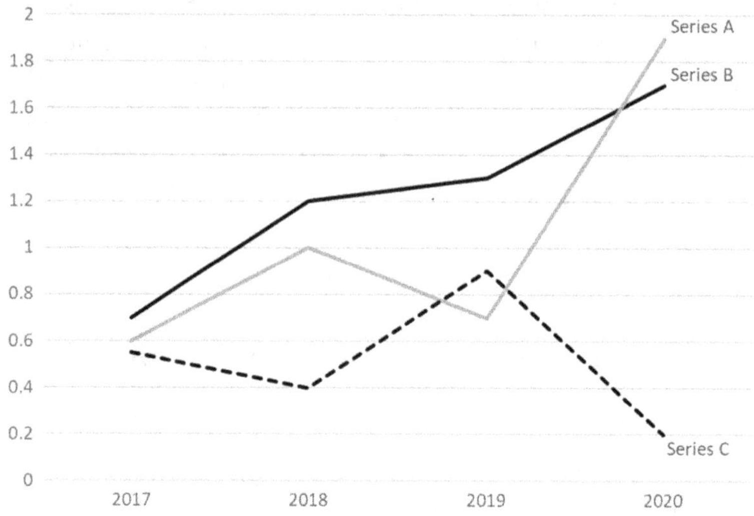

decreased), then they have a direct relationship. If the general trends for the two variables are different (i.e., one generally increased while the other generally decreased), then they have an inverse relationship.

5.2.3.2 *Writing the refinement*

Like the description of trends, we can look out for exceptions as a refinement. Using Figure 5.5 as an example, we see that while Series A and Series B have a generally direct relationship, there is an exception from 2018 to 2019 where they had an inverse relationship. From 2018 to 2019, while Series A fell, Series B increased.

5.2.4 *Worked examples*

In this section, we will go through a few worked examples. Each worked example is contrasted against the previous one(s) to show how changes in the data type, mark allocation, and content affect the answer. The worked examples are meant to be read in sequence so that these contrasts are clear.

Worked example 1

Figure 1: Maize price index (Base month = Oct-19)

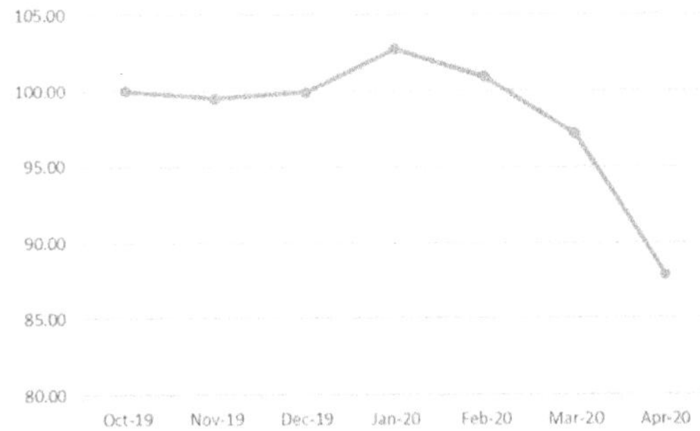

Source: indexmundi.com. Retrieved on 17 May 2020 from: https://www.indexmundi.com/commodities/?commodity=corn

(a) Using Figure 1, state what happened to the price of maize from Oct-19 to Apr-20. [2]

Ans: The price of maize generally decreased from Oct-19 to Apr-20 [1m] with an exception from Nov-19 to Jan-20 when it increased [1m].

Explanation of the answer:

- The command words "state what happened to" tells you that this is a "describe" question. The content and context are "the price of maize from Oct-19 to Apr-20". The additional condition is to use Figure 1.
- Since the content to be described is not a balance (it is a price index), the first mark goes to the general trend. You interpret the data to see that from the start to the end, the price had fallen overall.
- Since two marks are allocated, you need to include one refinement to earn the second mark. In this case, the exception is quite clear and you write it down.
- For help in interpreting indices, refer to the section "Interpreting indices" in Chapter 4.

Worked example 2

Table 1: Maize prices (% change from previous month)

Month	Nov-19	Dec-19	Jan-20	Feb-20	Mar-20	Apr-20
% change	–0.49	0.38	2.89	–1.79	–3.73	–9.55

Source: indexmundi.com. Retrieved on 17 May 2020 from: https://www.indexmundi.com/commodities/?commodity=corn

(*Continued*)

(*Continued*)

(a) Using Table 1, state what happened to the price of maize from Oct-19 to Apr-20. [3]

Ans: The price of maize generally decreased from Oct-19 to Apr-20 [1m] with an exception from Nov-19 to Jan-20 when it increased [1m]. Also, the sharpest reduction in price happened from Mar-20 to Apr-20 [1m].

Explanation of the answer:

- This question is like the one in worked example 1. The only differences are that the data type is changed and that the marks allocated are now 3 instead of 2.
- For the change in data type, refer to the section "Interpreting percentage change data" in Chapter 4 to see how it is interpreted.
- The extra mark allocated means that you need to include another refinement. The sharpest change in the same direction as the general trend is also quite clear and so you write it down.

Worked example 3

Figure 1: US trade in goods with China

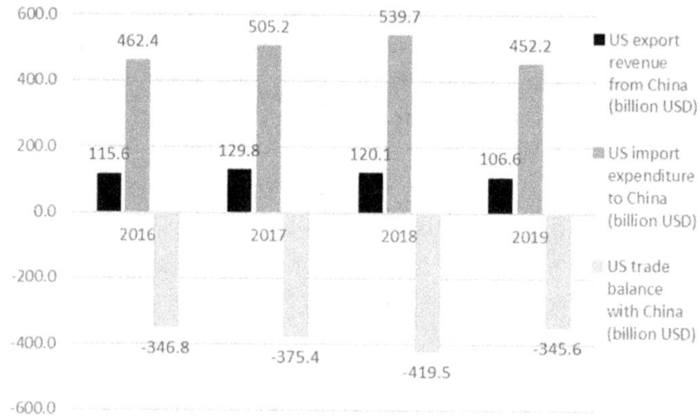

Source: United States Census Bureau. Retrieved on 17 May 2020 from: https://www.census.gov/foreign-trade/balance/c5700.html

(*Continued*)

(a) Describe the trend in the US balance of trade in goods with China shown in Figure 1. [3]

Ans: The US balance of trade in goods with China was in a deficit from 2016 to 2019 [1m]. Overall, the balance position improved [1m] except for 2016 to 2018 where it worsened [1m].

Explanation of the answer:

- The command word "describe" tells you that this is a "describe" question. From the content and context, you know you are only supposed to describe the balance of trade of US and so you ignore the irrelevant information of export revenue and import expenditure.
- Since the data is a balance (unlike the previous worked examples), the first mark goes to the statement of surplus/deficit.
- The second mark goes to the general trend. You can point out that the balance improved or that the deficit had decreased.
- Since three marks are allocated, there is still one more mark to earn. You earn it by writing the refinement — an exception in this case.
- For help in interpreting balances, refer to the section "Interpreting balances" in Chapter 4.

Worked example 4

Figure 1: Price of Arabica and Robusta Coffee (Base month = Oct-19)

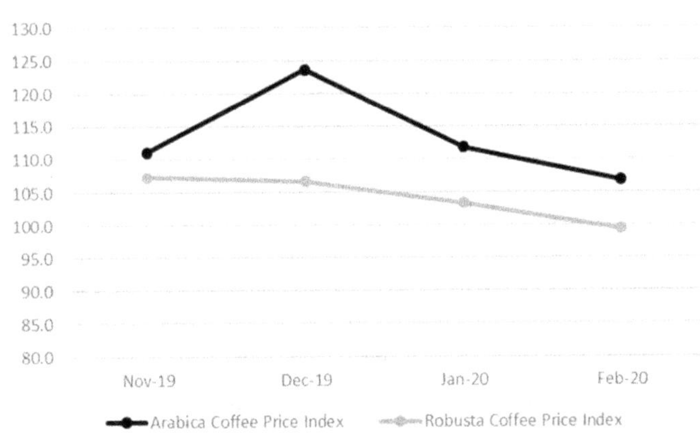

Source: indexmundi.com. Retrieved on 17 May 2020 from: https://www.indexmundi.com/commodities/?commodity=robusta-coffee&commodity=other-mild-arabicas-coffele

(*Continued*)

(*Continued*)

(a) With reference to Figure 1, describe the relationship between the price of Arabica and Robusta coffee. [2]

Ans: The prices of Arabica and Robusta coffee had a generally direct relationship [1m] although there was an exception from Nov 2019 to Dec 2019 where it was an inverse one [1m].

Explanation of the answer:

- The command word "describe" tells you that this is a "describe" question. The content, however, unlike the previous worked examples, is a relationship rather than a trend.
- Since we are describing a relationship, the first mark goes to the general relationship. We see that it's a direct one where for most of the time, the prices of the two type of coffee change together.
- The second mark goes to the refinement. Here, we can see a clear exception to the general direct relationship from Nov to Dec 2019 where the price of Arabica coffee increased while the price of Robusta coffee decreased.
- For help in interpreting price indices, refer to the section "Interpreting indices" in Chapter 4.

5.2.5 *Common pitfalls to avoid*

Common pitfalls that you should avoid include:

- **Reading the wrong data** — This could happen when the figure/table has more information than the question requires (e.g., the table/figure has more years of data or more trends than what you are supposed to describe). To avoid this, make sure you do your question analysis. The content and context of the 3C+ framework will help you to zoom in on what data to look at.
- **Misreading the percentage change data** — The percentage change data is a type of data that is used in case material often but is unfortunately also the most commonly misread data. So, be especially careful when you identify the data as percentage change data. You can refer to Section 4.4 in Chapter 4 to see how it is supposed to be interpreted.

5.3 *How to Answer a "Compare" (or a Synonym) Question*

A "compare" question is a question with the command word "compare" or a synonym of "compare". For example, the question "Compare the prices of Robusta Coffee and Arabica Coffee from Oct-19 to Apr-20" is a "compare" question as the command word is "Compare". The question "Contrast the prices of Robusta Coffee and Arabica Coffee from Oct-19 to Apr-20" is also a "compare" question because the command word "Contrast" is a synonym of "compare".

Examples of command words which tell you that the question is a "compare" question are presented in Table 5.9.

Although the command words are different, all three questions are asking for the exact same thing.

The content and context (in this case, "the prices of Robusta Coffee and Arabica Coffee from Oct-19 to Apr-20") tell you what you should be comparing and the additional condition, if provided, (in this case, "as shown in Figure 1") tells you where to find it. Note that while most "compare" questions require you to compare trends, it may not always be the case. The content to be compared could be relationships instead (e.g., "Compare the relationship between the price of Robusta Coffee and the price of Arabica coffee with that between the price of Robusta coffee and the price of rice from Oct-19 to Apr-20 shown in Figure 1").

Table 5.9: Command words which are synonymous with "compare".

Command Word/Phrase	Sample Question
Compare...	Compare the prices of Robusta Coffee and Arabica Coffee from Oct-19 to Apr-20 shown in Figure 1.
Contrast...	Contrast the prices of Robusta Coffee and Arabica Coffee from Oct-19 to Apr-20 shown in Figure 1.
State your observations about (2 or more sets of data)...	State your observations about the prices of Robusta Coffee and Arabica Coffee from Oct-19 to Apr-20 shown in Figure 1.

If the time period of observation (in this case "from Oct-19 to Apr-20") is not provided, then describe the entire range of data provided in the figure/table. Also, note that the figure/table might provide you with irrelevant data (e.g., provide you with the prices of three or more goods when the question only requires you to compare the prices of two goods). In such a scenario, be careful to not compare the wrong sets of data.

5.3.1 *Mark allocation*

"Compare" questions are marked by points. In general, each mark is awarded for a comparison in terms of whether the data is similar or different. A 1m "compare" question would require just one point of comparison; a 2m question would require two points of comparison; a 3m question would require three points of comparison and so on and so forth. However, what comparisons to prioritise depends on whether trends or relationships are being compared, and the type of data being compared (refer to Chapter 4 to see the different types of data).

5.3.1.1 *For comparing trends*

If the data to be compared are balances (e.g., balance of trade positions of two or more countries), the first mark is reserved for comparing the balance positions (i.e., surplus or deficit). The second mark (if it is a 2m question) is then awarded for comparing the general trend. Each subsequent mark, if any, is awarded for each further comparison provided. However, it is seldom that "compare" questions carry more than 2 marks.

If the data to be compared is not a balance (e.g., the prices of two or more goods), then it is not possible to have a comparison of balance positions. So, the first mark would be awarded for comparing the general trend and each subsequent mark is awarded for each further comparison provided. Usually, two comparisons are enough as it is seldom that "compare" questions carry more than 2 marks.

Table 5.10: Mark allocation for "compare" questions.

Compare...	
...two or more trends	**...two or more relationships**
First mark: Comparison of balance positions (Only applicable if the data to be compared are balances	First mark: Comparison of general relationships
Next mark: Comparison of general trend	Next mark: First further comparison
.	Next mark: Second further comparison
.	
Where to stop depends on how many marks are allocated	

5.3.1.2 *For comparing relationships*

Comparisons of relationships are seldom tested and will likely carry no more than one mark. This mark will be awarded for identifying whether the general relationships are similar or different (e.g., price levels and national output having a direct relationship whereas price levels and unemployment rates having an inverse relationship).

We summarise the mark allocation for "compare" questions in Table 5.10.

5.3.2 *How to answer it — Comparison of trends*

For each comparison, you must show whether it is a similarity or a difference by using words like "both" or "all" to show that there are similarities and use words like "however" or "while" to show that there are differences.

5.3.2.1 *(For balances only) Comparing the balance positions*

This is straightforward. If both (or all) of the balances are mostly positive or negative, then you would write that both (or all) of the balances were mostly in a surplus or deficit, which is a similarity. If one of the balances is mostly positive while the other(s) is mostly negative, then you would write that while one of the balance was mostly in a surplus, the other(s) was mostly in a deficit, which is a difference. It is also possible that one balance was mostly in a surplus/deficit while the other had some periods in which it had a surplus and others in which it had a deficit.

5.3.2.2 *Comparing the general trend*

Recall that the general trend refers to whether the value has increased or decreased overall. So, if both (or all) variables had increasing/decreasing trends, than that would be a similarity. If one had an increasing trend while the other(s) had the opposite, then that would be a difference.

Note that if the data is a balance, then we use the terms "improved/worsened" to describe the balance position instead of "increased/decreased". "Increased/Decreased" can be used, however, to describe the surplus/deficit (not the balance position). A surplus increasing means that the balance has become more positive and a deficit increasing means that the balance has become more negative. Table 5.11 summarises what phrasing is acceptable for comparing the general trend of balances.

You can refer to Chapter 4 to see how to interpret different types of data (e.g., percentage change data) to see if the value of the variable has increased/decreased so that you can compare the general trends.

Table 5.11: Summary of acceptable phrasing for comparing the general trend of balances.

Phrasing	Acceptable/Not Acceptable
Both balance positions (or just "balances") improved/worsened	Acceptable
Both balance positions (or just "balances") increased/decreased	Not acceptable
Both balance surpluses increased/decreased	Acceptable
Both balance deficits increased/decreased	Acceptable

Figure 5.6: Two items to be compared.

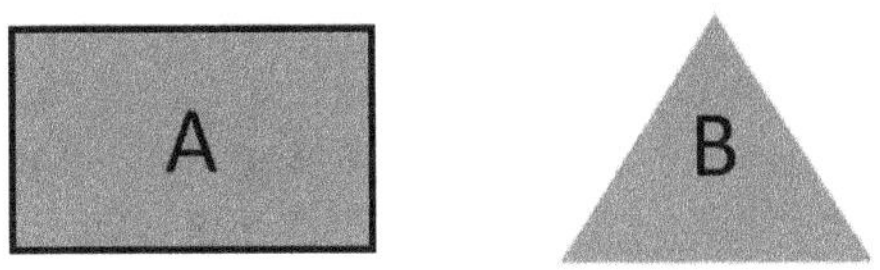

5.3.2.3 *Further comparisons*

Each further comparison you make should continue to be a like-for-like comparison. We use a non-economic example to illustrate what a like-for-like comparison. Let us imagine that you are asked to compare the two items in Figure 5.6.

You would not say that "Item A is a rectangle while item B is has no outline". That would not make sense. Instead, you would say "Item A is a rectangle while item B is a triangle" or "Item A has an outline while item B does not". This is because we must compare apples to apples. The categories of comparison in this case are the shapes of the items and whether the items have outlines. So, in this case, the points of comparison would be:

- Both items A and B have the same colour. (Similarity in terms of the category: colour.)
- Item A is a rectangle while item B is a triangle (Difference in terms of the category: shape.)
- Item A has an outline while item B does not. (Difference in terms of the category: whether there is an outline.)

Of course, in a case study question, the categories of comparison would not be colour or shape or whether the figure has an outline. Apart from the first two categories of balance position and general trend explained in the earlier sections, other categories you should use for further comparisons (if necessary) are:

- Extent of change
- Level

- Rate of change
- Variance

(a) **Extent of change** — Extent of change refers to how much the variable changed. We read this by seeing how much the variable changed from the start of the period to the end of the period (i.e., the gap between the first and last point). This is illustrated in Figure 5.7.

The example in Figure 5.7 shows that the extent of change is larger for the price of Arabica coffee than it is for Robusta coffee.

Note that the extent of change could be in absolute terms or percentage terms. Figure 5.6 shows the extent of change in absolute terms as we can see how much the prices had changed in terms of USD per kg. Percentage terms would be if we expressed the extent of change as a percentage of the original value. Using the price of Arabica coffee in Figure 5.7 as an example, the extent of change in absolute terms is about US$0.60 per kg (the price was about US$2.80 per kg in Oct-19 and was about US$3.40 per kg in Apr-20. The difference is US$0.60 per kg).

Figure 5.7: Coffee prices (USD per kg).

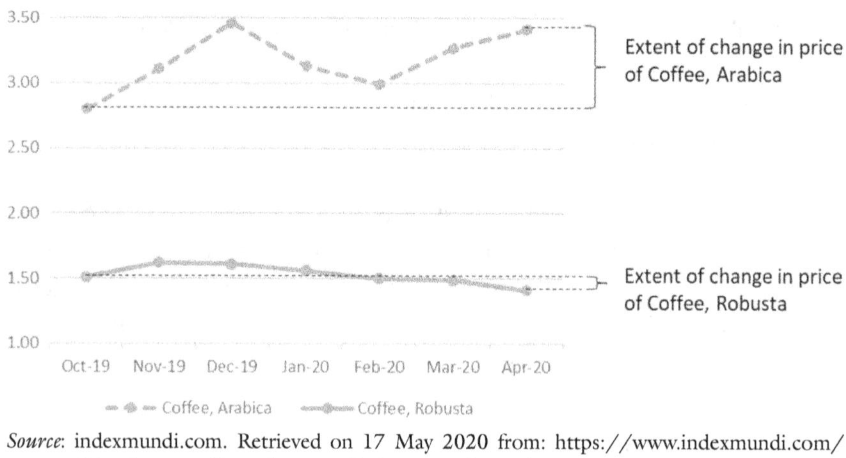

Source: indexmundi.com. Retrieved on 17 May 2020 from: https://www.indexmundi.com/commodities/?commodity=robusta-coffee&commodity=other-mild-arabicas-coffele

The extent of change in percentage terms would be about 21.43% (0.60/2.80 × 100%).

When you compare the extent of change, you should use the extent of change in percentage terms. However, if that is too time-consuming to calculate (possibly due to the graph being unclear), then you should make it clear in your answer that you are comparing the extent of change in absolute terms (e.g., write that "The change in the price of Arabica coffee was larger than that of Robusta coffee in absolute terms"). This is because by default, changes in economic variables are understood to be in percentage terms.

You can refer to Chapter 4 to see how to interpret the extent of change for different types of data (e.g., percentage change data).

(b) **Level** — The level refers to whether one set of data was consistently of a higher or lower value than the other set(s). For example, in Figure 5.7, the price of Arabica coffee ranged from about US$2.80 to US$3.40 per kg to while the price of Robusta coffee was always lower, ranging from about US$1.40 to US$1.50 per kg. So, we say that the price of Arabica coffee was at a higher level than the price of Robusta coffee.

The proper way to do this is to compare the average (Mathematical mean) values. The mean price of Arabica coffee is about US$3.17 per kg, which is indeed higher than that of Robusta coffee which is about US$1.53 per kg. However, in the A Level examinations, like in Figure 5.7, an eyeball test is usually more than enough to see which variable was at the higher level. Having said this, if this is not clear (e.g., if one set of data had higher values than the other set of data for some years but not for other others), then, instead of painstakingly calculating the mean values to determine which was higher on average, you should just use a different category of comparison.

Note that depending on the data type, you may not always be able to see the levels. For instance, if you are provided with two price indices, you cannot tell whether one good had a higher price than the other. The same goes for percentage change data. You can refer to Chapter 4 for more details of why this is so.

(c) **Rate of change** — To recap, the rate of change refers to whether the data is changing at an increasing rate (i.e., the changes are getting larger and larger) or at a decreasing rate (i.e., the changes are getting smaller and smaller) and not all data would have clear rates of changes. You can refer to Table 5.8 in the earlier section for details of how to interpret the rate of change.

If both (or all) sets of data have clear rates of change, then you can compare them and point out the similarities (if they all have increasing/decreasing rates of change) or differences (if one has an increasing rate of change while the other(s) has a decreasing rate of change).

For Figure 5.7, we would not use rate of change as one of the comparison points as neither the price of Arabica coffee nor the price of Robusta coffee had a clear rate of change.

(d) **Variation** — Variation refers to the degree of fluctuations in the data. A high variation means that the values swing a lot while a low variation means that the values are stable and do not change much. The variation is also known as the "spread" of values.

The proper way to compare the variance would be to calculate some measures of spread such as the statistical variance, the standard deviation, or the interquartile range and then compare these measures.[2] For example, the interquartile range for Arabica coffee is about US$0.29 per kg while that for Robusta coffee is about US$0.09 per kg. So, Arabica coffee has the greater variation in its values. However, just like with the comparison of levels, doing such calculations in an A Level examination setting is a clear overkill. Instead, you should simply do an eyeball check. For example, in Figure 5.7, we can see quite clearly that Arabica coffee prices have greater swings than Robusta coffee prices. So, even without calculating any measure of spread, we can make the comparison that Arabica coffee has the greater variation in its values.

When deciding which further comparison to write, choose the most salient (or most obvious) comparison. The extent of change is usually the most obvious but that is not always the case. For example, if one set of data had very large swings while the other was unusually stable, it may be better to point out the difference in variation instead.

5.3.3 *How to answer it — Comparison of relationships*

For the comparison of relationships, you need to first determine the relationships between variables before you can decide whether they are similar (e.g., the relationships are all direct) or different (one relationship is direct while the other(s) are inverse). Worked example 5 in Section 5.3.4 provides a good example.

5.3.4 *Worked examples*

In this section, we will go through a few worked examples. Each worked example is contrasted to the previous one(s) to show how changes in the data type and mark allocation affect the answer. The worked examples are meant to be read in sequence so that these contrasts are clear.

Worked example 1

Figure 1: Prices of maize and rice

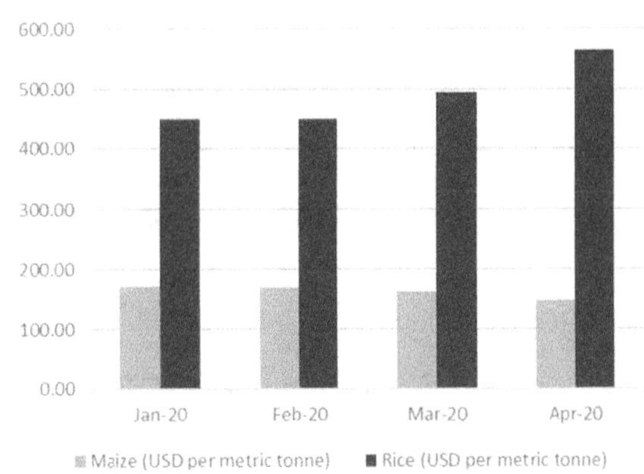

Source: indexmundi.com. Retrieved on 17 May 2020 from: https://www.indexmundi.com/commodities/?commodity=corn&commodity=rice

(a) Using Figure 1, compare the price of maize and rice from Jan-20 to Apr-20. [3]

Ans: The price of rice generally increased while the price of maize generally decreased from Jan-20 to Apr-20 [1m]. The extent of change was larger for the price of rice than for the price of maize in absolute terms [1m]. Finally, rice prices were consistently at a higher level than maize prices [1m].

(*Continued*)

(*Continued*)

Explanation of the answer:

- The command word "compare" tells you that this is a "compare" question.
- Since the data provided are not balances (they are prices), the first mark goes to comparing the general trend. In this case, we have a difference since one went up (increased) and the other went down (decreased).
- Since three marks are allocated, we need two other points of comparison.
    - o One comparison is the extent of change. We clarify that this is in absolute terms because while the price of rice seems to have changed more, the price of rice is also higher. So, we cannot be sure that the extent of change was larger for rice in percentage terms. Since it does not make sense to spend time calculating the actual percentage change to be sure, we just state that the difference in extent is in absolute terms.
    - o The other comparison is the level. We can do this because the data provided is absolute data (the units are in USD per metric tonne) so we know that the price of rice is indeed higher than that of maize.

Worked example 2

(a) Using Figure 1, compare the price of maize and rice from Jan-20 to Apr-20. [3]

Figure 1: Prices of maize and rice (Base month = Oct-19)

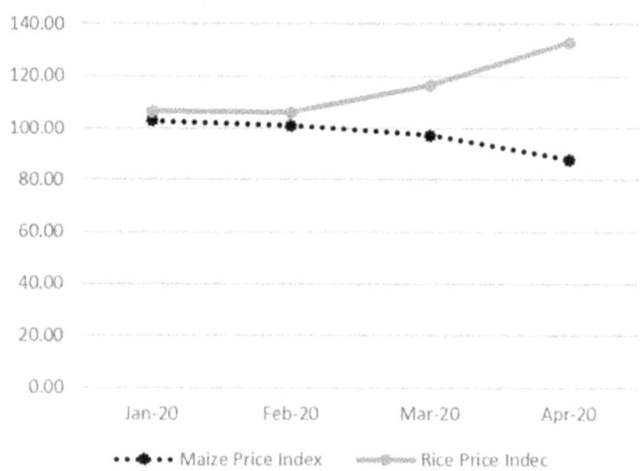

Source: indexmundi.com. Retrieved on 17 May 2020 from: https://www.indexmundi.com/commodities/?commodity=corn&commodity=rice

(*Continued*)

Ans: The price of rice generally increased while the price of maize generally decreased from Jan-20 to Apr-20 [1m]. The extent of change was larger for the price of rice than for the price of maize in [1m]. Finally, both prices seem to be changing at increasing rates [1m].

Explanation of the answer:

- This question is like the one in worked example 1. The only difference is that the data type is changed from absolute prices to price indices.
- With this data type, the second point of comparison (that the extent of the change in price of rice was larger than that of maize in absolute terms) is no longer valid. This is because price indices show the prices of each good as a percentage of its base year/month price. In this example, a price index of 101 for rice in Jan-20 and 102 in Feb-20 just means that the price of rice in Jan-20 was 101% of what it was in the base month (which is Oct-19, as stated in the title) and the price of rice in Feb-20 was 102% of what it was in the base month. So, while we know that the increase in the price of rice was 1% of the base month price, we have no way of knowing whether this was \$1 or \$2 or any other amount. Hence, we cannot compare the extent of change in absolute terms. We can, however, compare the extent of change in percentage terms. The extent of change in percentage terms is larger for rice that for maize as both price indices started at about 100 but the price index for rice rose to about 130 (so the percentage change is about 30%) but the price index for maize fell to about 85 (so the percentage change is about 15%). So, for the second point, we drop the words "in absolute terms" to show that the extent of change we are referring to is in percentage terms (recall that by default, extent of change is understood to be in percentage terms).
- Also, because of the change in data type, the third point of comparison (that the price of rice was at a higher level than that of maize) is no longer valid. This is again because price indices show the prices of each good as a percentage of its base year/month price. So, we cannot tell if the price of rice was indeed higher than that of maize. You can refer to the section "Interpreting indices" in Chapter 4 for more details.
- Since the third point of comparison is no longer valid, we need to replace it with another point of comparison. In this case, we can use the rate of change. Both trends seem to have increasing rates of change as the increases in the price of rice and the decreases in the price of maize both seem to be getting larger every month. This is a similarity.

Worked example 3

Table 1: Maize and rice prices (% change from previous month)

Month	Feb-20	Mar-20	Apr-20
Maize	–1.79%	–3.73%	–9.55%
Rice	–0.22%	9.78%	14.17%

Source: indexmundi.com. Retrieved on 17 May 2020 from: https://www.indexmundi.com/commodities/?commodity=corn&commodity=rice

(a) Using Table 1, compare the price of maize and rice from Jan-20 to Apr-20. [2]

Ans: The price of rice generally increased while the price of maize generally decreased from Jan-20 to Apr-20 [1m]. The extent of change was larger for the price of rice than for the price of maize [1m].

Explanation of the answer:

- This question is like the one in worked example 2. The only differences are that the data type is changed from price indices to percentage change from previous month, and that the mark allocation is lower (2m instead of 3m).
- Compared to worked example 2, the first comparison point about the general trend is still valid. You can refer to the section "Interpreting percentage changes" in Chapter 4 to see how the general trend is interpreted from percentage change data.
- The second comparison point about the extent of change is also still valid. Even with this percentage change data, it is quite clear that the extent of change in the price of rice is larger than that in the price of maize in percentage terms. The extent of change in the price of maize is approximately 15.07% (–1.79% + (–3.73%) + (–9.55%) = –14.07%) while that in the price of rice is approximately 23.73% (–0.22% + 9.78% + 14.17% = 23.73%).[3]
- Since the mark allocation is lower, we no longer need a third point of comparison.

Worked example 4

Table 1: US balance of trade in goods with selected EU economies (billion USD)

Year	2016	2017	2018	2019
France	–15.6	–15.3	–15.8	–19.7
Germany	–64.5	–63.6	–68.0	–67.2
UK	6.0	5.2	3.0	0.9

Source: United States Census Bureau. Retrieved on 20 May 2020 from: https://www.census.gov/foreign-trade/balance/index.html

(a) Contrast US's balance of trade in goods with each of the EU economies shown in Table 1. [2]

Ans: US had balance of trade deficits with France and Germany from 2016 to 2019 while it had surpluses with UK [1m]. The trade balances with every country worsened overall from 2016 to 2019 [1m].

Explanation of the answer:

- The command word "contrast" tells us that this is a "compare" question. From the content and context, we can see that this question differs from the previous worked examples because there are three balances to compare rather than two (which was the case for the earlier worked examples) and because the data to be compared are balances.
- Since the data provided are balances (unlike the previous worked examples), the first mark goes to the comparison of surplus/deficit. We also see that if there are more than two sets of data to compare, we point out which are similar (France and Germany in this case) and which is/are different (UK in this case).
- The second mark goes to the general trend. In this case, all the trade balances worsened since they became less positive/more negative overall. If some had improved and others had worsened, then we would point out which are similar and which is/are different in terms of whether their balance improved or worsened.
- Only 2 marks are allocated so two points of comparison are enough.

Worked example 5

Figure 1: Price of Rice, Arabica Coffee, and Robusta Coffee (Base month = Oct-19)

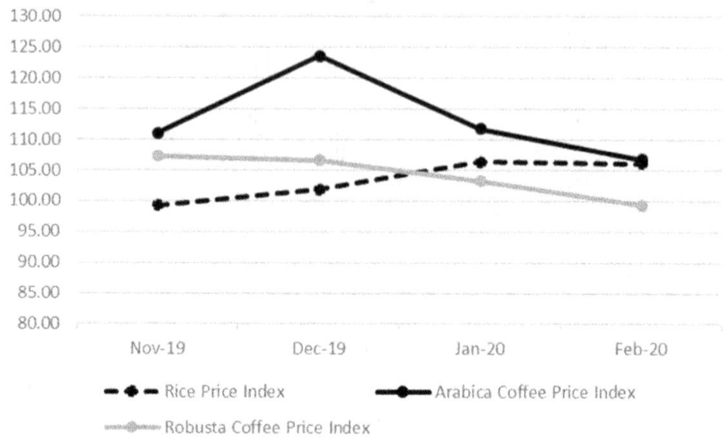

Source: indexmundi.com. Retrieved on 17 May 2020 from: https://www.indexmundi.com/commodities/?commodity=robusta-coffee&commodity=other-mild-arabicas-coffele and https://www.indexmundi.com/commodities/?commodity=rice

(a) With reference to Figure 1, compare the relationship between the price of Arabica and Robusta coffee with that between the price of Arabica coffee and the price of rice. [1]

Ans: The prices of Arabica and Robusta coffee had a generally direct relationship while the prices of Arabica coffee and rice had an inverse relationship [1m].

Explanation of the answer:

- The command word "compare" tells you that this is a "compare" question. The content to be compared, however, unlike the previous worked examples, are relationships rather than trends.
- Since we are comparing relationshipship, we must first identify the relationship that exist. We see that it's a direct one for the prices of the two type of coffees as they generally moved together. For the prices of Arabica coffee and rice, however, the relationship is an inverse one as they generally moved in opposite directions. Hence, we write down the difference in the relationships.
- For help in interpreting price indices, refer to the section "Interpreting indices" in Chapter 4.

5.3.5 *Common pitfalls to avoid*

Since comparison questions usually require comparisons of trends rather than relationships, the following common pitfalls apply mainly to comparisons of trends:

(a) **Insisting on finding a similarity and a difference** — A common misconception that students have is that "compare" questions have mark allocations of the first mark for a similarity and the second mark for a difference. As such, these students force themselves to identify similarities (or differences) even if they do not exist. Such effort is wrongheaded. There is no reason why there must be both similarities and differences. It is possible that both points of comparisons are similarities/differences. For example, an answer that states that "The US trade balance is in a deficit while China's is in a surplus. Also, the US trade balance is worsening while China's is improving" is a perfectly acceptable answer even though both points of comparison are differences between US's and China's balance of trade.

(b) **Only comparing subperiods** — Sometimes, two sets of data may have a similar trend except for a subperiod where one continued to increase while the other decreased (see example in Figure 5.8).

Figure 5.8: Example of a difference in only a sub-period.

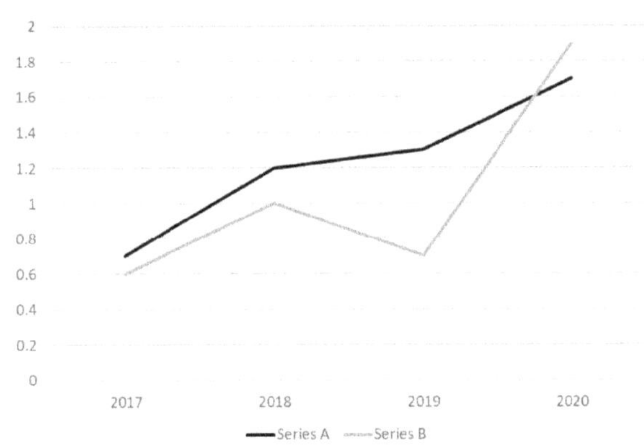

If the question were "Compare the trend in series A and B from 2017 to 2020" and carried two marks, many students would write that "Both Series A and Series B generally increased, but that from 2018 to 2019, Series A continued to increase while Series B decreased". The second comparison, "for 2018 to 2019, Series A continued to increase while Series B decreased" is problematic because it is a comparison of only a sub-period (2018–2019) when the question's context requires a comparison of the whole period (2017–2020). So, comparison points such as the extent of change over the whole period should be used instead (i.e., a better answer would be "Both Series A and Series B generally increased from 2017 to 2020. For this period, the extent of increase was larger for Series B").

(c) **Misreading percentage change data** — Percentage change data is the most commonly presented data type in case studies. Unfortunately, it is also the most commonly misinterpreted data type. So, be especially careful when you need to compare trends based on percentage change data. You can refer to Section 4.4 in Chapter 4 to see how percentage change data is supposed to be interpreted.

(d) **Misreading indices** — Students also often confuse indices with absolute data. This is relevant to comparisons of the level. For example, if you only have price indices, you cannot tell whether the price of one good is higher than another. You can refer to Section 4.3 in Chapter 4 to see how indices are supposed to be interpreted.

5.4 How to Answer a "Calculate" (or a Synonym) Question

A "calculate" question is a question with the command word "calculate" or a synonym of it.

Examples of command words which tell you that the question is a "calculate" question are presented in Table 5.12.

Table 5.12: Command words which are synonymous with "calculate".

Command Word/Phrase	Sample Question
Calculate...	Using information from Extract 1, calculate the price elasticity of demand (PED) for Fair Trade coffee.
Compute...	Using information from Extract 1, compute the price elasticity of demand (PED) for Fair Trade coffee.
Estimate...	Using information from Extract 1, estimate the price elasticity of demand (PED) for Fair Trade coffee.

Although the command words are different, all three questions are asking for the exact same thing.

The content and context (in this case, "the price elasticity of demand (PED) for Fair Trade coffee") tell you what you should be calculating and the additional condition, if provided, (in this case, "Using information from Extract 1") tells you where to find the information to do your calculation.

Also, note that the extract might provide you with irrelevant information (e.g., the change in the quantity demanded of a few goods when the question only requires you to calculate the price elasticity of demand (PED) of one good). In such a scenario, be careful to not use the wrong numbers for your calculation.

5.4.1 *Mark allocation*

"Calculate" questions are marked by points. If only one mark is allocated, an accurate final answer is enough. If two marks are allocated, then one mark would be for providing the correct formula before you provide the final answer. This is summarised in Table 5.13.

Note that there is no need to express the answer to three significant figures. Use what is sensible. For example, if what you need to calculate is in USD, then clearly the answer should be to two decimal points (e.g., US$1.50) or be rounded off to the nearest dollar.

Table 5.13: Mark allocation for "calculate" questions.

Calculate...
First mark: Correct answer
Next mark: Correct formula
A "calculate" question will not be more than two marks unless there are more than two things to be calculated. If so, the above mark allocation would apply to each item to be calculated.

5.4.2 *How to answer it*

The calculations that you can be tested on will be based on formulas that you learn in the A Level Economics syllabus. Once you know which formula you should be using, use it to get your answer. The calculation is usually straightforward in that it normally only involves one operation (i.e., an addition or subtraction or multiplication or division). Include the formula if necessary (i.e., if it is a 2m calculation question).

A list of the common formulas required is presented in Table 5.14. These are presented in order of frequency of being tested.

Table 5.14: List of common formulas in Economics.

Concept(s)	Formula and Example
Price elasticity of demand (PED)	$\text{PED} = \frac{\%\Delta \text{ in Quantity demanded of a good } (Q_D)}{\%\Delta \text{ in Price of the good } (P)}$ E.g., if a 2% increase in price of apple juice causes a 3% fall in the quantity demanded of apple juice, then $\lvert\text{PED}\rvert_{\text{apple juice}} = -1.5\ (-3\%/2\%)$
Income elasticity of demand (YED) [not in H1 Economics 8843 syllabus]	$\text{YED} = \frac{\%\Delta \text{ in Quantity demanded of a good } (Q_D)}{\%\Delta \text{ in Income } (Y)}$ E.g., if a 2% increase in consumers' incomes causes a 3% rise in the quantity demanded of apple juice, then $\lvert\text{YED}\rvert_{\text{apple juice}} = 1.5\ (3\%/2\%)$

Table 5.14: (*Continued*)

Concept(s)	Formula and Example
Cross elasticity of demand (XED) [not in H1 Economics 8843 syllabus]	$\text{XED} = \dfrac{\%\Delta \text{ in Quantity demanded of a good } A\ (Q_{DA})}{\%\Delta \text{ in price of another good } B\ (P_B)}$ E.g., if a 2% increase in the price of orange juice causes a 3% rise in the quantity demanded of apple juice (because consumers switch to buying apple juice), then $\lvert\text{XED}\rvert_{\text{apple juice}}$ = 1.5 (3%/2%)
Price elasticity of supply (PES)	$\text{PES} = \dfrac{\%\Delta \text{ in Quantity supplied of a good } (Q_S)}{\%\Delta \text{ in Price of the good } (P)}$ E.g., if a 2% increase in the price of apple juice causes a 3% rise in the quantity supplied of apple juice, then $\lvert\text{PES}\rvert_{\text{apple juice}}$ = 1.5 (3%/2%)
Real and nominal growth	Real growth = Nominal growth – Inflation rate Note that "growth" is just another term for percentage change E.g., if nominal GDP increased by 5% and the inflation rate was 2%, then the real GDP increased by 3% (5% – 2%). We could also phrase it as "the real GDP growth was 3%"
Real and nominal interest rate	Real interest rate = Nominal interest rate – Inflation rate E.g., if the nominal interest rate is 5% and the inflation rate was 2%, then the real interest rate is 3% (5% – 2%)
Balance of Trade (BOT) [not in H1 Economics 8843 syllabus]	BOT = Export revenue (X) – Import expenditure (M) E.g., If a country collects $100 million in export revenue but spent $150 million on import expenditure in the period, then the BOT for this country would be –$50 million ($100 million – $150 million) for that period.
Government budget balance	Budget balance = Government revenue or Tax revenue (T) – Government expenditure (G) E.g., If the government of a country collects $100 million in taxes in 2020 but spent $150 million in the same year, then the budget balance for this country would be –$50 million ($100 million – $150 million) for that year.
...per capita/head/ person	(variable) per capita = (variable)/Population size E.g., If a country has a real GDP of $100 million and there are 25 million people in the country, then the real GDP per capita would be $4 ($100 million/25 million)
...per capita growth	(variable) per capita growth = (variable) growth – Population Growth E.g., if real GDP increased by 5% and the population grew by 2%, then the real GDP per capita increased by 3% (5% – 2%). We could also phrase it as "the real GDP per capita growth was 3%"

5.4.3 *Worked examples*

In this section, we will go through a few worked examples. Each worked example is contrasted to the previous one(s) to show how a change in mark allocation affects the answer. The worked examples are meant to be read in sequence so that the contrast is clear.

Worked example 1

Extract 1: The price elasticity of demand of Fair Trade coffee

Demand for Fair Trade certified products has been continuously growing during the past decade. In 2008 the sales of all Fair Trade products grew by 57%, showing the strong growth in this market. Fair Trade is a voluntary certification system, where certain conditions are set on the production of mainly agricultural products. Fair Trade goods produced according to the Fair Trade criteria are guaranteed a minimum price above the world market price, as well as a social premium on top of the price.

The topic of interest, the price elasticity of demand of Fair Trade coffee, can be interpreted from the results of the research. According to researchers, a 1% increase in the price of the Fair Trade coffee causes a 0.5% decrease in kilogram sales. As such, a rise in price will have such a small effect on the drop in demand that the total revenue will rise.
Source: Adapted from Niemi (2009).

(a) Using information from Extract 1, calculate the price elasticity of demand (PED) for Fair Trade coffee. [1]

Ans: The PED of Fair Trade coffee is –0.5 [1m].
Explanation of the answer:

- The command word "calculate" tells you that this is a "calculate" question.
- Since only one mark is allocated, the final answer will suffice. We get the answer –0.5 by dividing –0.5% (fall in kilogram sales, which is the quantity demanded of Fair Trade coffee) by 1% (the increase in price of Fair Trade coffee).

Worked example 2

Extract 1: The price elasticity of demand of Fair Trade coffee

Demand for Fair Trade certified products has been continuously growing during the past decade. In 2008 the sales of all Fair Trade products grew by 57%, showing the strong growth in this market. Fair Trade is a voluntary certification system, where certain conditions are set on the production of mainly agricultural products. Fair Trade goods produced according to the Fair Trade criteria are guaranteed a minimum price above the world market price, as well as a social premium on top of the price.
The topic of interest, the price elasticity of demand of Fair Trade coffee, can be interpreted from the results of the research. According to researchers, a 1% increase in the price of the Fair Trade coffee causes a 0.5% decrease in kilogram sales. As such, a rise in price will have such a small effect on the drop in demand that the total revenue will rise.
Source: Adapted from Niemi (2009).

(a) **Using information from Extract 1, calculate the price elasticity of demand (PED) for Fair Trade coffee. [2]**

Ans: PED of Fair Trade coffee $= \dfrac{\%\Delta \text{ in } Q_D \text{ of Fair Trade coffee}}{\%\Delta \text{ in Price of Fair Trade coffee}}$ [1m].

The PED is –0.5%/1% = –0.5 [1m].

Explanation of the answer:

- This question is like the one in worked example 1. The only difference is that the mark allocation is higher.
- The extra mark allocated explains why we included the formula before doing the calculation and presenting the answer.

5.4.4 *Common pitfalls to avoid*

Common pitfalls that you should avoid include:

(a) **Problems with the negative sign** — This applies more to calculations of elasticities. You must remember that an increase is a positive percentage change while a decrease is a negative percentage change. For example, in the worked examples, the rise in price was 1% while the fall in quantity demanded was –0.5%. Many students have the tendency to only divide 0.5% by 1% to get a PED of 0.5. This would be wrong since the PED should be –0.5. So, if the calculation is for an elasticity, you should be very careful with the sign.

The problem of a negative sign sometimes affects the calculation of balances too. Students tend to want to subtract the smaller number from the larger number. For example, if export revenue were $10 million and import expenditure were $18 million, some students would want to subtract $10 million from $18 million. This would give a trade balance of $8 million, which would be wrong as the trade balance should be calculated using X – M, which would give us –$8 million. Familiarity with the formulas is necessary to avoid such errors.

(b) **Not recognising quantity demanded** — This is also a problem more specific to calculations of elasticities. While the percentage change in price is usually clear, the quantity demanded may not be. This is because case materials seldom use the terms "quantity demanded". Terms like "sales" may be used instead (like in Extract 1 of the worked examples). The term "demand" may also be used in layman fashion to stand for quantity demanded.

5.5 How to Answer a "Identify"/"Suggest" Question

An "identify" question is a question with the command word "identify" or a synonym of it. A "suggest" question is a question with the command word "suggest" or a synonym of it.

These two questions have slightly different requirements. However, they will be explained together because they have several similarities too.

Examples of question phrases which tell you that the question is an "identify" question or a "suggest" question are presented in Table 5.15.

Table 5.15: Command words which are synonymous with "identify" and "suggest".

Sample Question Phrases for an "Identify" Question	Sample Question Phrases for a "Suggest" Question
State the evidence that shows…	Propose…
State which product/economy…	State what could be a possible reason/factor for…
Based on Extract 1, what might have accounted for…	Based on the case material and/or your own knowledge, what might have accounted for…

You should notice that for these two question types, the command word alone does not tell you whether it is an "identify" or "suggest" question. For example, from the second row of Table 5.15, the command word for both types of question is "state".

Instead, the distinguishing factor between the two is whether you need to pick out points from the case material (for "identify" questions) or are you allowed to use your own knowledge (for "suggest" questions). This can be seen in the third row of Table 5.15 where the only difference between the question phrasing for the two question types is whether the additional condition ("Based on…") directed you to only use the case material or allowed you to use your own knowledge.

This also means that if a question is phrased as "With reference to Extract 1, suggest a reason for…", it is an "identify" question since the reason must be identified from Extract 1. This is so even though the command word is "suggest".

In summary, "identify" questions require you to pick out something from the case material while "suggest" questions do not. What you suggest could be from your own knowledge.

5.5.1 *Mark allocation*

Both question types are marked by points, with each mark allocated to each thing identified/suggested. For example, if a question is "Identify the reasons for the increase in the price of rice" and carries two marks, then each reason identified would be worth one mark each.

Table 5.16: Mark allocation for "identify"/"suggest" questions.

Identify...	**Suggest...**
First mark: One item identified Next mark: Another item identified . . Where to stop depends on how many marks are allocated and how many items are required to be identified by the questions	First mark: First suggestion Subsequent mark(s): Subsequent suggestion(s) or explanation of first suggestion (depends on how many suggestions the question requires compared to how many marks are allocated)

Similarly, a question like "Suggest two reasons for the increase in the price of rice" should also be worth two marks, with one mark allocated to each suggested reason. If it carries more marks, then you are also expected to explain these reasons (how to answer "explain" questions is covered in a later section). To be fair, if you are supposed to suggest reasons and explain them, the question's phrasing should be "Suggest and explain two reasons for the increase in the price of rice". However, case study questions are set by humans which leaves room for errors.

The mark allocations for both question types are summarised in Table 5.16.

Most of the time, "identify" or "suggest" questions carry no more than two marks. The mark allocation could be higher if they were combined with other command words (e.g., "Identify and explain the reasons for the slowdown in global economic growth"). Such questions with two or more command words will be covered in the later section titled "How to answer a question with multiple command words".

5.5.2 *How to answer it*

5.5.2.1 *For "identify questions"*

To answer "identify" questions, you need to understand the case material and pull out the relevant information. For instance, if you are asked to identify factors/reasons for something (e.g., the reasons for an increase in exports of a country), then you should look for the causes of that thing in the extracts. You may also be asked to identify something from the numerical data (e.g., which country had the highest growth rate or which product was the closest substitute for another product), which would require you to understand the numerical data. In short, identification questions become easily answered when you understand the case study material. The skills to help you understand case study material were covered in Chapters 3 (for understanding the textual case material such as the extracts) and Chapter 4 (for understanding the numerical case material such as tables of numbers and figures).

5.5.2.2 *For "suggest" questions*

To answer "suggest" questions, you need to have a strong understanding of the economic content. For example, you must know the factors of demand and supply so that, if you are asked to suggest reasons for a change in either, you can recall the factors from memory. The case material may or may not be helpful.

5.5.3 *Worked examples*

In this section, we will go through a few worked examples. Each worked example is contrasted to the previous one(s) to show how a change in mark allocation affects the answer and how the answer for a "suggest" question differs from an "identify" question. The worked examples are meant to be read in sequence so that the contrast is clear.

Worked example 1

Extract 1: China exports rebound in April, but outlook remains grim

China's exports unexpectedly rose in April for the first time this year as factories raced to make up for lost sales due to the coronavirus shock, but a double-digit fall in imports signals more trouble ahead as the global economy sinks into recession.

(*Continued*)

(*Continued*)

Overseas shipments in April rose 3.5 per cent from a year earlier, marking the first positive growth since December last year, customs data showed on Thursday. The increase was driven in part by rising exports of medical equipment, traditional Chinese medicine and textiles, which include masks. China exported millions of tonnes of medical products worth 71.2 billion yuan (S$14.2 billion) in the March–April period, according to the customs agency. The daily export value of medical supplies jumped by more than three times last month.

Some economists also attributed the rise in exports to factory closures elsewhere, leading to a surge in import demand, just as China's manufacturers reopened after extended shutdowns due to the virus outbreak.

Source: *The Straits Times*, 7 May 2020. Retrieved on 15 May 2020 from: https://www.straitstimes.com/business/economy/china-exports-see-surprise-gain-in-april-but-rebound-seen-as-temporary

(a) With reference to Extract 1, identify a reason for the "positive growth" in China's exports. [1]

Ans: One reason is the rising exports of medical equipment, traditional Chinese medicine and textiles [1m].

Explanation of the answer:

- The command word "identify" tells you that this is an "identify" question.
- Since only one mark is allocated (and because the question phrasing is "a reason"), we just need to pick out a reason from the case study material. The phrase "driven by" in the second paragraph tells us that the "rising exports of medical equipment, etc." is a reason. You can refer to Chapter 3 to see how to understand the information in extracts.

Worked example 2

Extract 1: China exports rebound in April, but outlook remains grim

China's exports unexpectedly rose in April for the first time this year as factories raced to make up for lost sales due to the coronavirus shock, but a double-digit fall in imports signals more trouble ahead as the global economy sinks into recession.

(*Continued*)

Overseas shipments in April rose 3.5 per cent from a year earlier, marking the first positive growth since December last year, customs data showed on Thursday. The increase was driven in part by rising exports of medical equipment, traditional Chinese medicine and textiles, which include masks. China exported millions of tonnes of medical products worth 71.2 billion yuan (S$14.2 billion) in the March–April period, according to the customs agency. The daily export value of medical supplies jumped by more than three times last month.

Some economists also attributed the rise in exports to factory closures elsewhere, leading to a surge in import demand, just as China's manufacturers reopened after extended shutdowns due to the virus outbreak.

Source: *The Straits Times*, 7 May 2020. Retrieved on 15 May 2020 from: https://www.straitstimes.com/business/economy/china-exports-see-surprise-gain-in-april-but-rebound-seen-as-temporary

(a) With reference to Extract 1, identify the reasons for the "positive growth" in China's exports. [2]

Ans: One reason is the rising exports of medical equipment, traditional Chinese medicine and textiles [1m]. The other reason is the closure of factories elsewhere [1m].

Explanation of the answer:

- This question is like the one in worked example 1. The only difference is that the mark allocation is higher (and the phrasing is now "reasons" rather than "a reason").
- Since one more mark is allocated, we need to identify another reason. The phrase "attributed the rise in exports to" in the third paragraph tells us that the "factory closures elsewhere" is a reason too. You can refer to Chapter 3 to see how to understand the information in extracts.

Worked example 3

Extract 1: China exports rebound in April, but outlook remains grim

China's exports unexpectedly rose in April for the first time this year as factories raced to make up for lost sales due to the coronavirus shock, but a double-digit fall in imports signals more trouble ahead as the global economy sinks into recession.

(*Continued*)

(*Continued*)

Overseas shipments in April rose 3.5 per cent from a year earlier, marking the first positive growth since December last year, customs data showed on Thursday. The increase was driven in part by rising exports of medical equipment, traditional Chinese medicine and textiles, which include masks. China exported millions of tonnes of medical products worth 71.2 billion yuan (S$14.2 billion) in the March–April period, according to the customs agency. The daily export value of medical supplies jumped by more than three times last month.

Some economists also attributed the rise in exports to factory closures elsewhere, leading to a surge in import demand, just as China's manufacturers reopened after extended shutdowns due to the virus outbreak.

Source: *The Straits Times*, 7 May 2020. Retrieved on 15 May 2020 from: https://www.straitstimes.com/business/economy/china-exports-see-surprise-gain-in-april-but-rebound-seen-as-temporary

(a) Suggest three possible reasons for the "positive growth" in China's exports (Extract 1). [3]

Ans: One reason could be the rising exports of medical equipment, traditional Chinese medicine and textiles [1m]. The other reason could be the closure of factories elsewhere [1m]. A third possible reason could be that some countries were experiencing earlier recoveries and hence starting to purchase more of China's exports [1m].

Explanation of the answer:

- This question is like the one in worked example 2 except that the command word is now "suggest" and the mark allocation is higher.
- You will notice that the first two reasons suggested still came from the extract. This is because the command word "suggest" does not mean that you cannot use the case material. It only means that you could provide possible points from beyond the case material such as the third suggested reason, which was provided because the question phrasing specified "three reasons" and the 3 marks are allocated.
- Note that the "(Extract 1)" simply means that the quotation was from Extract 1, not that you need to refer to Extract 1. If you were supposed to do so, the question phrasing would have included the additional

(*Continued*)

condition of "Using Extract 1" or "With reference to Extract 1" or something to that effect.

This is an atypical question that is included to illustrate a learning point. Most of the time, "identify" and "suggest" questions carry no more than 2 marks.

Worked example 4

Extract 1: China exports rebound in April, but outlook remains grim

China's exports unexpectedly rose in April for the first time this year as factories raced to make up for lost sales due to the coronavirus shock, but a double-digit fall in imports signals more trouble ahead as the global economy sinks into recession.

Overseas shipments in April rose 3.5 per cent from a year earlier, marking the first positive growth since December last year, customs data showed on Thursday. The increase was driven in part by rising exports of medical equipment, traditional Chinese medicine and textiles, which include masks. China exported millions of tonnes of medical products worth 71.2 billion yuan (S$14.2 billion) in the March–April period, according to the customs agency. The daily export value of medical supplies jumped by more than three times last month.

Some economists also attributed the rise in exports to factory closures elsewhere, leading to a surge in import demand, just as China's manufacturers reopened after extended shutdowns due to the virus outbreak.

Source: *The Straits Times*, 7 May 2020. Retrieved on 15 May 2020 from: https://www.straitstimes.com/business/economy/china-exports-see-surprise-gain-in-april-but-rebound-seen-as-temporary

(a) Suggest a possible reason for the "positive growth" in China's exports (Extract 1). [3]

Ans: One reason could be the rising exports of medical equipment, traditional Chinese medicine and textiles [1m]. The coronavirus shock caused a rise in demand for medical equipment to treat patients suffering from the virus and of traditional Chinese medicine and masks (textiles) as people

(*Continued*)

(*Continued*)

try to stay safe and healthy [1m]. The increase in demand for these goods produced by China caused an increase in China's export revenue as an increase in demand causes both the price and output of these goods exported by China to increase [1m].

Explanation of the answer:

- This question is like the one in worked example 3 except that now only one reason is required even though the mark allocation is 3 marks.
- Since the suggestion of a reason should only carry 1 mark, the remaining 2 marks allocated tells us that an explanation is required.
- Most explanations require some application of an economic model (the demand and supply model in this case). Explanations will be covered in proper detail in the later section "How to answer an "Explain" (or a synonym) question".

5.5.4 *Common pitfalls to avoid*

There is only one common error to avoid — Confusing "identify" questions with "suggest" questions. Other errors will be due to not understanding the case material (and therefore not being able to do the "identify" question) or not having the required economic content knowledge (and therefore not being able to do the "suggest" question).

5.5.4.1 *Confusing "identify" questions with "suggest" questions*

Thinking that a "suggest" question is an "identify" question could lead to a waste of time combing the case material for things that may not be present. Thinking that an "identify" question is a "suggest" question could lead to answers that are irrelevant because the correct case material was not referred to. To avoid this, interpret the question carefully and literally. For example, if the question states that you can "use your own knowledge", then you may. Or, if the question states that you should provide "possible" reasons, then any plausible reason is acceptable. It need not be from the case material. Of course, if the question tells you to refer to the case material, then you should follow that too.

5.6 How to Answer an "Infer"/"Interpret" Question

An "infer" question is a question with the command word "infer" or a synonym of it. Similarly, an "interpret" question is a question with the command word "interpret" or a synonym of it.

"Infer" and "interpret" are not exactly synonyms. However, they will be lumped together because this book is getting too long and more importantly, they both require you to make meaning out of the case material.

Examples of command words which tell you that the question is a "infer/interpret" question are presented in Table 5.17.

Although the command words are different, all three questions are asking for the exact same thing.

The content and context (in this case, "South Korea's population growth") tell you what you should be interpreting and the additional condition, if provided, (in this case, "Table 1") tells you where to find the information to do your inference/interpretation.

Table 5.17: Command words which are synonymous with "infer/interpret".

Command Word/Phrase	Sample Question
What can be inferred from...	From Table 1, what can be inferred about South Korea's population growth?
What does (the data) show about...	What does Table 1 show about South Korea's population growth?
Interpret...	Interpret what Table 1 shows about South Korea's population growth.

5.6.1 *Mark allocation*

"Infer/Interpret" questions are marked by points. Each inference/interpretation carries one mark. However, each inference/interpretation must include some explanation. If there is clearly only one inference/interpretation to be made but more than one mark allocated, then the extra marks will be allocated to providing more detail in the explanation. This idea of providing more details for a given explanation when more marks are allocated is the concept of "zooming in". Conversely, for a given explanation, if fewer marks are allocated, we "zoom out" and provide fewer details. "Zooming in" and "zooming out" will be further explained in later sections. The mark allocation for "infer/interpret" questions is summarised in Table 5.18.

Note that the marking scheme in Table 5.18 is on the more stringent end of things. It is possible that for some years, the question requirement may be less demanding and the inference/interpretation without any explanation may be awarded one mark. However, it is always better to provide more detail in your answer than less.

5.6.2 *How to answer it*

Generally, the inferences/interpretations fall in into two categories. You either need to infer/interpret something from manipulating some numbers or from understanding economic indicators (e.g., Gini coefficient).

Table 5.18: Mark allocation for "infer/interpret" questions.

Infer/Interpret...
First mark: First inference/interpretation (includes some explanation) Next mark: Next inference/interpretation (includes some explanation) OR Explanation of the first inference/interpretation (if there is clearly only one inference/interpretation to be made) . . Where to stop depends on how many marks are allocated.

5.6.2.1 *Inferences/Interpretations based on manipulating numbers*

Making inferences/interpretations based on manipulating numbers in the tables/figures requires the same skillset as a "calculate" question.

You must first understand how to read the data provided (you can refer to Chapter 4 to see how this is done) and understand the relevant formula to use (you can refer to a list of the common formulas used in A Level Economics in Table 5.14 in the earlier section titled "How to answer a "Calculate" (or a synonym) question").

The most common inference to be made involves per capita figures and uses the formulas:

- (variable) per capita = (variable)/Population size, or
- (variable) per capita growth = (variable) growth – Population Growth.

Using either formula, you can see that so long as you know the change in two out of the following three things (the variable, the population, and the variable per capita), you can infer the third thing. For example, if you know that the GDP had increased and that the population had decreased, then both formulas would tell you that the GDP per capita must have increased. In this case, GDP is the variable.

For the first formula, the increase in GDP would be an increase in the numerator on the right side of the equation. The decrease in population is a decrease in its denominator. If the numerator increases while the denominator decreases, then the fraction must increase. Therefore, the GDP per capita must increase.

For the second formula, the increase in the GDP means that the GDP growth is a positive number. The decrease in the population means that the population growth is a negative number. So, the growth in the GDP per capita must be a positive number since it is equal to a positive number – a negative number. A positive GDP per capita growth means that GDP per capita increased.

If the above is all too confusing, you can always plug in real or hypothetical numbers to see how the value of the variable you need to infer will change.

Remember to provide a brief explanation of how you obtained your inference.

5.6.2.2 *Inferences/Interpretations based on understanding economic indicators*

The other type of inference/interpretation is based on understanding economic indicators. For instance, you may be asked to interpret what an increase in the Gini coefficient means. To answer this, you need to know what the Gini coefficient measures (extent of income inequality) and how it is to be read (0 for perfect equality to 1 for perfect inequality). With this understanding, you will be able to interpret the increase in the Gini coefficient to mean that incomes have become more unequally distributed. A list of common indicators and how they are interpreted is provided in Table 5.19.

You should notice that for elasticities, the interpretation will always involve two parts — interpretation of the sign and interpretation of the magnitude.

Table 5.19: Common indicators.

Indicator	What Does It Measure?	How to Read It?
Gini coefficient	• Income inequality	• 0 for perfect equality • 1 for perfect inequality • The higher the number, the more unequally incomes are distributed • Is sometimes scaled 0 to 100 instead
Human Development Index (HDI)	• Overall well-being in terms of education and healthcare for non-material aspects of standards of living, and GNI per capita for material aspects of standards of living	• Goes from 0 to 1 (or scaled 0 to 100) • The higher the number, the greater the overall well-being • Individual aspects of education, healthcare, and GNI per capita cannot be compared as they are all aggregated to give one figure

Table 5.19: (*Continued*)

Indicator	What Does It Measure?	How to Read It?
Price elasticity of demand (PED)	• Degree of responsiveness of quantity demand to a change in price, ceteris paribus	• Sign: ○ Negative sign means that quantity demanded and price have an inverse relationship • Magnitude: ○ |PED| > 1 means that the demand for the good is price elastic ○ |PED| < 1 means that the demand for the good is price inelastic
Income elasticity of demand (YED) [not in H1 Economics 8843 syllabus]	• Degree of responsiveness of quantity demand to a change in income, ceteris paribus	• Sign: ○ Positive sign means that quantity demanded and income have a direct relationship (i.e., good is a normal good) ○ Negative sign means that quantity demanded and income have an inverse relationship (i.e., good is an inferior good) • Magnitude: ○ |YED| > 1 means that the demand for the good is income elastic. Good is either a luxury good or a very inferior good ○ |PED| > 1 means that the demand for the good is income inelastic. Good is either a necessity or a slightly inferior good
Cross elasticity of demand (XED) [not in H1 Economics 8843 syllabus]	• Degree of responsiveness of quantity demand to a change in price of another good, ceteris paribus	• Sign: ○ Positive sign means that the quantity demanded of the good and the price of the other good have a direct relationship (i.e., the two goods are substitutes) ○ Negative sign means that the quantity demanded of the good and the price of the other good have an inverse relationship (i.e., the two goods are complements) • Magnitude: ○ |XED| > 1 means that the demand for the good is cross elastic. The goods are ether close substitutes or close complements

(*Continued*)

Table 5.19: (*Continued*)

Indicator	What Does It Measure?	How to Read It?
		○ $\|XED\| < 1$ means that the demand for the good is cross inelastic. The goods are ether weak substitutes or weak complements
Price elasticity of supply (PES)	• Degree of responsiveness of quantity supplied to a change in price, ceteris paribus	• Sign: ○ Positive sign means that quantity supplied and price have a direct relationship • Magnitude: ○ $\|PES\| > 1$ means that the supply for the good is price elastic ○ $\|PED\| < 1$ means that the supply for the good is price inelastic

For each interpretation, remember to provide a brief explanation of how you got it.

5.6.3 *Worked examples*

In this section, we will go through a few worked examples. Each worked example is contrasted to the previous one(s) to show how a change in mark allocation or other parts of the question affects the answer. The worked examples are meant to be read in sequence so that the contrast is clear.

Worked example 1

Table 1: Economic indicators of South Korea (annual % change)

	2016	2017	2018
Real GDP	0.9	0.8	2.4
Population	0.4	0.3	0.5

Source: World Bank Databank (2020). Retrieved on 23 May 2020 from: https://databank.worldbank.org/reports.aspx?source=2&country=KOR

(*Continued*)

(a) Using Table 1, infer the change in South Korea's real GDP per capita from 2016 to 2018. [1]

Ans: South Korea's real GDP per capita increased from 2016 to 2018 as the real GDP increased by a greater extent than the population [1m].

Explanation of the answer:

- The command word "infer" tells you that this is an "infer" question.
- Since only one mark is allocated, the inference itself and a brief explanation will suffice. We get the answer from comparing the growth of real GDP against the growth of the population. In each of the years, the real GDP increased by a larger extent than the population (we see this from the fact that the percentage change for real GDP was always higher than that of the population). So, the real GDP per capita, or the average real GDP, must have increased.

Worked example 2

Table 1: Economic indicators of South Korea (annual % change).

	2016	**2017**	**2018**
Real GDP	0.9	0.8	2.4
Population	0.4	0.3	0.5

Source: World Bank Databank (2020). Retrieved on 23 May 2020 from: https://databank.worldbank.org/reports.aspx?source=2&country=KOR

(a) Using Table 1, infer the change in South Korea's real GDP per capita from 2016 to 2018. [2]

Ans: South Korea's real GDP per capita increased from 2016 to 2018 as the real GDP increased by a greater extent than the population [1m]. The greater extent of the increase in real GDP can be seen from the percentage change for real GDP and population both being positive, with the former being higher than the latter [1m].

(*Continued*)

(*Continued*)

Explanation of the answer:

- This question is like the one in worked example 1. The only difference is that the mark allocation is higher.
- The extra mark allocated explains why we provided further explanation of how we got the inference.

Worked example 3 [not in H1 Economics 8823 syllabus]

Table 1: Elasticities of demand for soft drinks in Chile.

Elasticity of demand for soft drinks with respect to:	**Value**
Price of soft drinks	–1.37
Price of plain water	0.63

Source: Adapted from Guerrero-López, Unar-Munguía, and Colchero (2017).

(a) Using Table 1, interpret the value of the elasticity of demand for soft drinks with respect to the price of water. [2]

Ans: The value of the elasticity of demand for soft drinks with respect to the price of water (i.e., the cross elasticity of demand (XED) for soft drinks) is 0.63. Since it is a positive number, an increase in the price of plain water would cause an increase in the quantity demanded for soft drinks. As such, the two must be substitutes [1m]. However, as the |XED| is less than one, the increase in quantity demanded of soft drinks would be less than proportionate to the increase in the price of water (i.e., cross inelastic). Hence, they are only weak substitutes [1m].

Explanation of the answer:

- The command word is "interpret" and the content to be interpreted is the XED. So, we ignore the PED of soft drinks that is provided.
- This question is like the one in worked example 2 in that they are both 2-mark questions. However, while worked example 2's mark allocation was 1m for the inference and 1m for the explanation, here, both marks are for the interpretations. This is because for elasticities, there are always two things to be interpreted — the sign and the magnitude.

5.6.4 *Common pitfalls to avoid*

Students are more likely to trip over infer/interpret questions when the content to be inferred/interpreted is a per capita figure or an elasticity concept.

5.6.4.1 *Problem with inferring per capita figures*

Students sometimes get confused about whether they should divide one thing by another or subtract one thing from another. For example, if the real GDP growth is 3% and the population growth is 5%, some students would think that the real GDP per capita would grow by 0.6% (from 3/5). Since this is a positive number, they would then infer that the real GDP per capita increased. This is wrong because since these figures are growth rates, the correct formula to use should have been real GDP per capita growth = real GDP growth – population growth. If we use this formula, then the real GDP per capita growth is –2%, which means that real GDP per capita shrank. To avoid this sort of problem, students must remember that there are two formulas related to "per capita" and which to use depends on what data you have. We will use real GDP per capita as the example:

- Formula 1: real GDP per capita = real GDP/population (use if real GDP and population are raw data)
- Formula 2: %Δ in real GDP per capita = %Δ in real GDP – %Δ in population (use if real GDP and population data provided are %Δs (i.e., growth rates))

The above formulas would also apply to other "per capita" figures such as labour productivity (i.e., output per worker).

You can refer to Chapter 4 to see how to read the different types of data.

5.6.4.2 *Problem with elasticity values*

Students sometimes also trip over interpreting elasticity values. Most students will interpret the magnitude in terms of whether the demand or supply is price elastic, but many tend to forget to interpret the sign. The interpretations of the sign of the elasticity values were in Table 5.19 shown earlier.

5.7 How to Answer a "Define" Question

A "define" question has the command word "define". There are also other ways to phrase a define question that are shown in Table 5.20.

Although the command words are different, all three questions are asking for the exact same thing.

5.7.1 *Mark allocation*

"Define" questions are marked by points. Each accurate definition carries one mark. Note that there may be more than one term to defined in a question. For example, for "Define real GDP", there are two terms to be defined — "real" and "GDP". So, such a "define" question could carry two marks instead. Having said that, it is also possible that the paper is a demanding one and only one mark is allocated even though there are two terms to be defined.

If more than one mark is allocated, then something more than a definition would need to be provided. This extra something could be an example or a formula (if relevant) or a brief explanation of how the thing to be defined is used.

The important thing to note is simply this — a definition will only carry one mark and any marks beyond that would mean that either there is another term to be defined, or that something extra such as an example is required. This is summarised in Table 5.21.

It is very unlikely that a "define" question would carry more than two marks.

Table 5.20: Command words which are synonymous with "define".

Command Word/Phrase	Sample Question
Define...	Define real GDP.
State the definition of...	State the definition of real GDP
What does...mean?	What does "real GDP" mean?

Table 5.21: Mark allocation for "define" questions.

Define...
First mark: Provision of definition
Next mark: Provision of definition of other term OR an example of the first term (if there is no other term to be defined)

5.7.2 *How to answer it*

There is no way around it — definitions must be memorised. While word-for-word regurgitation may not be necessary, the key words/ phrases in the definition must be accurate. So, unless your command of English is masterful, it may simply be easier to memorise definitions as they are.

5.7.3 *Worked examples*

In this section, we will go through a few worked examples. Each worked example is contrasted to the previous one(s) to show how a change in mark allocation or other parts of the question affects the answer. The worked examples are meant to be read in sequence so that the contrast is clear.

Worked example 1

(a) Define real gross domestic product (GDP). [2]

Ans: Real GDP is the total monetary value of all final goods and services produced within the geographical boundary of a country in a year [1m] calculated using base year prices [1m].

Explanation of the answer:

- The command word is "define" and the content to be defined is "real GDP".
- Since there are two terms that need a definition here ("real" and "GDP"), the definition of each term carries one mark.
- Since the mark allocation is just two marks, there is no need to provide anything beyond the definitions.

Worked example 2

(a) Define gross domestic product (GDP). [2]
Ans: GDP is the total monetary value of all final goods and services produced within the geographical boundary of a country in a year [1m]. It can be calculated using base year prices to give real GDP or current prices to give nominal GDP [1m].

Explanation of the answer:

- This question is like the one in worked example 1. The only difference is that there is only one term to be defined ("GDP") but the mark allocation is still two marks.
- Since the definition of GDP only carries one mark, we need to provide something extra to earn the other mark. In this case, we provided more details about how it can be calculated. It is also possible to earn this second mark by providing examples or further explanations of what GDP is.

5.7.4 *Common pitfalls to avoid*

For definition questions, the main problem student face is that they sometimes remember the definition wrongly or incompletely. This is especially so for longer definitions where some parts of the definition tend to be left out (e.g., the "ceteris paribus" in each of the elasticity definitions). To overcome this, when memorising definitions, try to memorise them by parts and take note of how many parts there are.

5.8 How to Answer an "Explain" (or a Synonym) Question

An "explain" question has the command word "explain". There are also other ways to phrase a define question that are shown in Table 5.22.

Although the command words are different, all three questions are asking for the exact same thing. Technically, according to Bloom's taxonomy that ranks the difficulty of tasks (if you are a regular student taking A Level Economics, you can ignore this bit), "analyse" is a higher-order command word than "explain". However, for the A

Table 5.22: Command words which are synonymous with "explain".

Command Word/Phrase	Sample Question
Explain...	Explain the increase in the price of petroleum-based products.
Analyse...	Analyse the increase in the price of petroleum-based products.
Why...?	Why did the price of petroleum-based products increase?

Level Economics examinations, the requirements for both are not very much different (if at all).

5.8.1 *Mark allocation*

"Explain" questions are marked by points. Each point is awarded for a step in the explanation. The more marks there are, the more steps there must be in the explanation or the more parts to the explanation there must be. Additionally, if the question explicitly requires a diagram (e.g., the question phrasing states "With the aid of a diagram"), marks would be allocated for the diagram. For H2 Economics (9757 syllabus), the diagram always only carries one mark. For H1 Economics (8823 syllabus), it could carry up to two marks depending on how complex the diagram is. Note that diagram marks are only awarded if the diagram is referenced to in the explanation. All of these are summarised in Table 5.23.

Table 5.23: Mark allocation for "explain" questions.

Explain...
First mark: First step of the explanation
Next mark: Next step of the explanation
.
.
Last mark: Last step of the explanation
For H2 Economics (9570 syllabus): One of the marks could be for a referenced diagram.
For H1 Economics (8843 syllabus): One or two of the marks could be for a referenced diagram, depending on how complex the diagram is.

5.8.2 *How to answer it*

Most "explain" questions require an explanation of cause-and-effect. There are some exceptions and we will consider them under the last chapter on dealing with unusual questions. For now, we will focus on the typical "explain" questions that require cause-and-effect explanations. To find the cause and effect, we will need to look at the content to be explained as well as the context of the question.

The steps to answering such questions are to:

Step 1: Identify the cause and effect
Since most "explain" questions require cause-and-effect explanations, the first step is naturally to determine what the cause(s) and effect(s) are. Let's take a look at an example.

Example 1: Explain how "an expanding middle class" (Extract 1) caused meat prices to increase.

In the above example, the cause is "an expanding middle class" and the effect is an increase in meat prices. This is straightforward.

However, not all questions are so straightforward. Sometimes, there may be multiple causes and/or multiple effects. There could also be cases where the cause/effect is hidden. We will show these cases in the next few examples.

Example 2 (multiple causes): Explain how "an expanding middle class" (Extract 1) and the "culling of livestock" (Extract 2) caused meat prices to increase.

In Example 2, we see that there are now two causes and one effect. The two causes are "an expanding middle class" and "culling of livestock". The effect is still just an increase in meat prices. Both causes are contributing to the same effect.

Example 3 (multiple effects): Explain how "an expanding middle class" (Extract 1) caused meat prices to increase but canned food prices to fall.

In Example 3, there is now one cause (the "expanding middle class") and two effects — the rise in price of meat and the fall in the price of canned food.

Example 4a (hidden cause(s)): With reference to Extract 1, explain why meat prices increased.

In Example 4a, something must have caused the price of meat to increase. So, while the effect is clear (the effect is an increase in the price of meat), the cause(s) is not. For such cases, the cause(s) is likely to be from the case material. For this example specifically, the cause(s) should be found in Extract 1.

Example 4b (hidden cause(s)): Explain a possible reason for why meat prices increased.

Example 4b is similar to example 4a in that the effect is an increase in the price of meat but the cause is not given. However, it differs from example 4a as example 4a requires the cause to be found from Extract 1 while for example 4b, the phrase "possible reason" means that the cause could be a theoretical one (i.e., need not be from the case material).

Example 5 (hidden effect(s)): With reference to Extract 1, explain the effects of "an expanding middle class" (Extract 1).

In Example 5, the cause is apparent — "an expanding middle class" but the effect is not explicitly stated. For such cases, the effect(s) is likely to be from the case material and in this example specifically, the effect(s) should be found in Extract 1.

Questions that have hidden causes are quite common but those with hidden effects are quite rare. Nonetheless, whichever it is, for "explain" questions, we should first identify the cause(s) and effect(s).

Step 2: Unpack the effect in economic terms
After identifying the cause(s) and effect(s), the next step is to interpret the effect(s) in terms of economic variables. The term "economic variables" was introduced in Chapter 3 (Section 3.3.2). To recap, economic variables are the things we study in economic models such as price, quantity, real GDP, and the general price level. Some examples are provided in Table 5.24 where the effect is in **bold** type and the interpretation of the effect is in the column next to it.

The examples in Table 5.24 are basic. However, in the exam, the effects to be explained may not always be so straightforward. For example, in the question "Explain how "the oil price shock" (Extract 1) caused a food crisis", the effect is "a food crisis". We

Table 5.24: Examples of interpretation of effects.

Question Phrasing	Interpretation of the Effects
Explain the **change in the price of rice**.	A change in price of rice (i.e., P_{rice}).
Explain the **change in the output of rice**.	A change in the quantity traded of rice (i.e., Q_{rice}). *Note*: We assume that the consumption/production of rice is the equilibrium quantity consumed/produced, both of which give us the equilibrium quantity traded.
Explain the **change in rice consumption**.	
Explain the **change in rice production**.	

Table 5.24: (*Continued*)

Question Phrasing	Interpretation of the Effects
Explain the **change in consumer expenditure on rice.** Explain the **change in revenue of rice producers.**	A change in ($P_{rice} \times Q_{rice}$). *Note*: Consumer expenditure on a good and producer revenue from the good must have the same numerical value since what the consumer spends must be what the producer receives.
Explain the **effect on the market for rice.**	A change in P_{rice} and a change in Q_{rice} (e.g., P_{rice} increasing and Q_{rice} decreasing). *Note*: If the mark allocation is high enough, we may also need to provide the change in consumer expenditure/total revenue.
Explain why the **market for healthcare fails.** Explain why **governments need to intervene in the market for healthcare.**	Inefficiency and/or inequity (more likely inefficiency) in the market. *Note*: The reason for government intervention must be that the market has failed. *Note*: For H1 Economics (8823 syllabus), the market failure only includes inefficiency but not inequity.
Explain the **change in (a firm's) profit.**	A change in profit, which is the same as a change in (total revenue – total cost).
Explain the **change in the real GDP of Singapore.**	A change in real $NY_{Singapore}$.
Explain the **change in Singapore's consumer price index (CPI).**	A change in real $GPL_{Singapore}$.
Explain the **change in Singapore's unemployment rate.**	A change in the unemployment rate.

would need to look at the case material (and use our common sense) to determine what "a food crisis" means in terms of economic variables. This and some other examples where the effect is more ambiguous are presented in Table 5.25.

Table 5.25: Examples of ambiguous effects and how to interpret them.

Question Phrasing	Interpretation of the Effects
Explain how "the oil price shock" (Extract 1) caused **a food crisis.**	Presumably, a food crisis describes a situation where people cannot afford food. This means that food prices must have increased and so the interpretation is a rise in P_{food}.
Explain how government policies have led to **"prosperity for all"** (Extract 1).	"Prosperity for all" means that everyone has gotten richer. We could interpret this as an increase in real GDP per capita, which also implies an increase in real GDP (assuming the population remained unchanged).

We can see that even for ambiguous phrasing, we should still interpret the effects in terms of changes in economic variables (food price and real GDP for the two examples above). And, to do so, we should use both the case material and our common sense.

If the effect is still unclear after reading the case material and applying your common sense, it is best to write down what your interpretation of the effect is before you write the explanation. This is so that you have a chance of earning some marks even if your interpretation is a little off the mark.

Step 3: Determine the economic model to apply

Once we have interpreted the effect(s) in terms of economic variables, we select the appropriate model to explain the change in the economic variable. For the A Level Economics examination, an economic model can be thought of as a graph (e.g., the demand and supply model, the aggregate demand and aggregate supply model, the firm model (only for H2 Economics 9570 syllabus)). To determine which model is appropriate, we need a good understanding of what each economic model does. For example, since the demand and supply model is meant to explain the changes in price and quantity traded in an industry, when we need to explain a change in price and/or change in quantity traded in an industry, we would naturally require the demand and supply model.

Examples of which effects require the use of which models are presented in Table 5.26.

Table 5.26: Selecting the appropriate model to apply.

If You Need to Explain a Change in...	Examples of Questions	Model to Apply
• Market price of a good • Quantity traded of a good in the market • Any economic variable that involves the price and/or quantity traded in the market (e.g., total revenue, which is P × Q)	Explain the fall in the price of wheat from 2000 to 2010. Explain the trend in consumer spending on apparel observed in Figure 1. Explain how deglobalisation would affect the tourism sector.	Demand and supply model *Note*: The terms "market", "industry", and "sector" are mostly interchangeable. When the analysis is of a change in P and/or Q at this level, the model to apply is the demand and supply model. *Note*: Elasticities are a part of the demand and supply model. They are applied if there is a need to explain the extent of the change in P and/or Q.
• Efficiency	Explain how the presence of "spillover effects" (Extract 1) causes market failure. Explain why governments must intervene when "consumers may not know what is good for them" (Extract 1).	Market failure models (e.g., externalities, imperfect information, etc.) *Note*: Not all market failure models are illustrated using graphs. Public goods, asymmetric information (only in H2 Economics 9570 syllabus) are two examples of market failure that are not illustrated on graphs.
[Not applicable to H1 Economics 8843 syllabus] • Price charged by a firm • Output of a firm • Any economic variable that involves the price and/or output of a firm (e.g., profit, which is TR – TC or (PxQ) – TC)	[Not applicable to H1 Economics 8843 syllabus] Explain how "stronger brand loyalty" (Extract 1) allowed Apple to increase the price of its products. Explain the trend in Amazon's profits shown in Table 1. Explain how "ever cheaper pesticides" (Extract 1) would affect the price and output decision of a coffee farmer.	[Not applicable to H1 Economics 8843 syllabus] Firm model (i.e., the graph with AR, MR, AC, and MC curves) *Note*: The firm model and the demand and supply model seem to be similar as they both explain changes in P and Q. The difference is that the demand and supply model explains changes in P and Q in the market (e.g., change in price of smartphones in general) whereas the firm model explains changes in the P and Q of a firm (i.e., change in the price of iPhones produced by Apple, a specific smartphone firm).

(*Continued*)

Table 5.26: (*Continued*)

If You Need to Explain a Change in...	**Examples of Questions**	**Model to Apply**
• Real GDP • GPL • Unemployment (demand-deficient)	Explain the reasons for Singapore "slipping into a technical recession" (Extract 1). Explain why the US economy is expected to experience "gloomy skies ahead" (Extract 1). Explain how Covid-19 would affect the Chinese economy.	Aggregate demand and aggregate supply (AD–AS) model *Note:* Almost all effects on an economy are analysed using the AD–AS model.

Figure 5.9: Structure of answering an explain questions.

Step 4: Link the cause to the economic model and then to the effect

Once we have determined the cause(s), the effect(s), and which economic model to apply, we can write the answer. The answer should start with the cause, link the cause to the economic model, and then link the economic model to the effect. This is illustrated in Figure 5.9.

How much detail to provide would depend on the mark allocation. The higher the mark allocation, the more detail to provide (i.e., "zoom in" and provide more details) and the lower the mark allocation, the fewer details are required (i.e., "zoom out" and provide fewer details).

We will go through the above steps (including "zooming in" and "zooming out") in the worked examples in the next section. The worked examples cover both microeconomic and macroeconomic topics so that you can see how the skills are the same regardless of the topics.

5.8.3 *Worked examples*

In this section, we will go through a few worked examples. Each worked example is contrasted to the previous one(s) to show how a change in mark allocation or other parts of the question affects the answer. The worked examples are meant to be read in sequence so that the contrast is clear.

Worked example 7 is from a macroeconomic topic to show that the skills are transferable.

Worked example 1

Extract 1: Chinese consumers grapple with 'flying pigs' as food inflation soars

When it comes to buying food for daily meals, Chinese consumers are increasingly being forced to swallow unaffordable prices for a staple product — so-called flying pigs.

Supply-side problems have sent the price of pork surging this year, with the price trend becoming a fixture of local media reporting in the process.

Last month, pork prices rose by 85.7 per cent on-year and expanded 10.3 per cent from June, new data from the National Bureau of Statistics showed. The price of pork has more than doubled in the first seven months of the year from the same period in 2019.

Pork prices are rising because the stock of hogs and breeding sows are still recovering from the African Swine Fever epidemic that hit the country in late 2018, according to the government. The coronavirus pandemic and recent flooding in central and southern China have also hurt supply.

Meanwhile, demand for pork has risen quickly as more restaurants have resumed their business after nationwide coronavirus lockdowns early in the year.

(*Continued*)

(*Continued*)

Many Chinese consumers are starting to feel the pinch and some have been forced to cut back on purchases of the staple goods.

Source: Adapted from *South China Morning Post*, 10 Aug 2020. Retrieved on 19 August 2020 from: https://www.scmp.com/economy/china-economy/article/3096777/chinese-consumers-grapple-flying-pigs-and-rocketing-eggs

(a) Analyse how "supply-side problems" (Extract 1) are affecting the market for pork in China. [3]

Ans:
The "supply-side problems" refer to the slow recovery of hogs and breeding sows stocks, the coronavirus pandemic, and flooding in China. The latter two cause a fall in supply that outweighs the small increase in supply from the first factor. This causes an overall fall in the supply of pork. [1m] This then causes a shortage and hence an upward pressure on the price of pork. As pork price increases, the shortage shrinks as the quantity demanded would fall and the quantity supplied would rise until eventually a new equilibrium is reached. [1m] Overall, price of pork would rise but quantity traded would fall. [1m]

Explanation of the answer:

- Since the command word "analyse" is a synonym of the command word "explain", this is an "explain" question and we can apply our steps.
- Step 1: Identify the cause and effect — In this case, the cause is "supply-side problems" and the effect is the effect on the "market for pork in China".
- Step 2: Unpack the effect in economic terms — The effect on the "market for pork in China" is interpreted to mean the effect on the market price of pork (whether it rises or falls) and the effect on the quantity traded in the market (whether it rises or falls).
- Step 3: Determine the economic model to apply — Since the effect to be explained is a change in price and quantity traded in a market, the model to apply is the demand and supply model.

(*Continued*)

- Step 4: Link the cause to the model and then to the effect — In this case, we want to do the following:

  "supply-side problems"→ $\underbrace{\text{fall in supply overall}}_{\text{Demand and supply model}}$ → ↑P and ↓Q

We notice that there does not seem to be very much to explain for the three marks allocated. So, we need to "zoom in" on the explanation and provide more detail (which is why the complete price adjustment process is included in the answer).

Worked example 2

Extract 1: Chinese consumers grapple with 'flying pigs' as food inflation soars

When it comes to buying food for daily meals, Chinese consumers are increasingly being forced to swallow unaffordable prices for a staple product — so-called flying pigs.

Supply-side problems have sent the price of pork surging this year, with the price trend becoming a fixture of local media reporting in the process.

Last month, pork prices rose by 85.7 per cent on-year and expanded 10.3 per cent from June, new data from the National Bureau of Statistics showed. The price of pork has more than doubled in the first seven months of the year from the same period in 2019.

Pork prices are rising because the stock of hogs and breeding sows are still recovering from the African Swine Fever epidemic that hit the country in late 2018, according to the government. The coronavirus pandemic and recent flooding in central and southern China have also hurt supply.

Meanwhile, demand for pork has risen quickly as more restaurants have resumed their business after nationwide coronavirus lockdowns early in the year.

Many Chinese consumers are starting to feel the pinch and some have been forced to cut back on purchases of the staple goods.

(*Continued*)

(*Continued*)

Source: Adapted from *South China Morning Post*, 10 Aug 2020. Retrieved on 19 August 2020 from: https://www.scmp.com/economy/china-economy/article/3096777/chinese-consumers-grapple-flying-pigs-and-rocketing-eggs

(a) With the aid of a diagram, analyse how "supply-side problems" (Extract 1) are affecting the market for pork in China. [3]

Ans:

The "supply-side problems" refer to the slow recovery of hogs and breeding sows stocks, the coronavirus pandemic, and flooding in China. The latter two cause a fall in supply that outweighs the small increase in supply from the first factor. This causes an overall fall in the supply of pork. [1m].

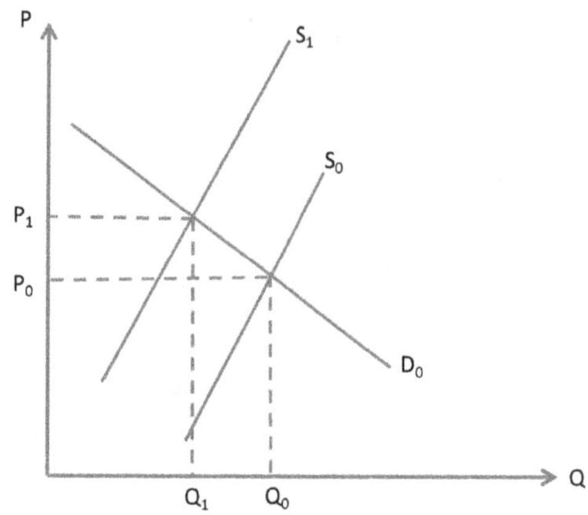

As shown in the diagram above [1m], as supply falls from S_0 to S_1, a shortage is created, causing price to increase from P_0 to P_1. The quantity traded would also fall from Q_0 to Q_1. [1m]

Explanation of the answer:

- This question is like the one in worked example 1. The only difference is that it now requires a diagram.

(*Continued*)

- Since the diagram will be worth 1m (this is also true for H1 since it is a simple diagram with just one curve shifting), it means that the explanation only carries two marks. So, in step 4, we "zoom out" and provide fewer details in the explanation. Note that even when details are dropped, what the cause is, which model is being used, and what the effects are must still be kept.
- Also, because diagram marks are only awarded when there is a reference to the diagram, we make sure that we describe the diagram in our explanation.

Worked example 3

Extract 1: Chinese consumers grapple with 'flying pigs' as food inflation soars

When it comes to buying food for daily meals, Chinese consumers are increasingly being forced to swallow unaffordable prices for a staple product — so-called flying pigs.

Supply-side problems have sent the price of pork surging this year, with the price trend becoming a fixture of local media reporting in the process.

Last month, pork prices rose by 85.7 per cent on-year and expanded 10.3 per cent from June, new data from the National Bureau of Statistics showed. The price of pork has more than doubled in the first seven months of the year from the same period in 2019.

Pork prices are rising because the stock of hogs and breeding sows are still recovering from the African Swine Fever epidemic that hit the country in late 2018, according to the government. The coronavirus pandemic and recent flooding in central and southern China have also hurt supply.

Meanwhile, demand for pork has risen quickly as more restaurants have resumed their business after nationwide coronavirus lockdowns early in the year.

Many Chinese consumers are starting to feel the pinch and some have been forced to cut back on purchases of the staple goods.

(*Continued*)

(*Continued*)

Source: Adapted from *South China Morning Post*, 10 Aug 2020. Retrieved on 19 August 2020 from: https://www.scmp.com/economy/china-economy/article/3096777/chinese-consumers-grapple-flying-pigs-and-rocketing-eggs

(a) With the aid of a diagram, analyse how "supply-side problems" and restaurants resuming their business (Extract 1) are affecting the market for pork in China. [5]

Ans:
The "supply-side problems" refer to the slow recovery of hogs and breeding sows stocks, the coronavirus pandemic, and flooding in China. The latter two cause a fall in supply that outweighs the small increase in supply from the first factor. This causes an overall fall in the supply of pork. [1m]. At the same time, as restaurants resume their business, there would be an increase in demand for pork as people start eating out and consuming more pork as opposed to what they would consume at home. [1m]

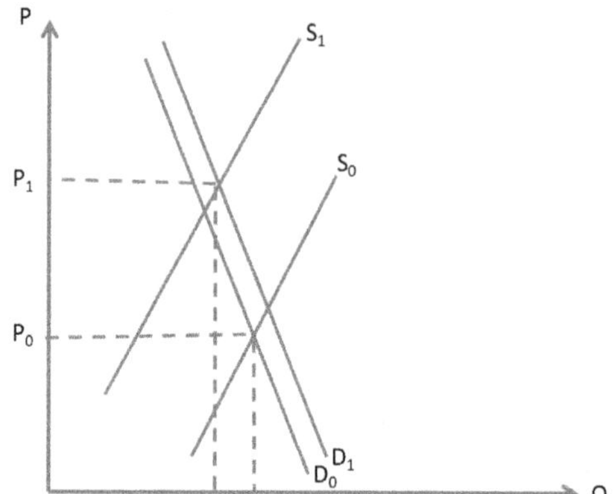

As shown in the diagram above [1m], as supply falls from S_0 to S_1 and demand increases from D_0 to D_1, a shortage is created, causing price to increase from P_0 to P_1. [1m] Whether the quantity traded increases or decreases depends on whether the decrease in supply outweighs the increase in demand. Assuming it does, the quantity traded would fall from Q_0 to Q_1. [1m]

(*Continued*)

Explanation of the answer:

- This question is like the one in worked example 2. The only differences are that there are now two causes instead of one, and that the mark allocation is higher.
- Because there are now two causes instead of one, step 4 would be:

"supply-side problems" → fall in supply overall → ↑ P and ↓ Q (assuming change in supply is larger)

restaurants resuming business → rise in demand

Demand and supply model

We can see that both causes are linked to the economic model before it is linked to the effects. Also, although there are more marks, we do not zoom in to provide more details because the additional marks are for including the additional cause and including the explanation that the change in quantity traded would depend on the relative extent of shifts.

Note: This would have been a 6m question for H1 as the diagram would have been worth 2m since it had two curves shifting simultaneously.

Worked example 4

Extract 1: Chinese consumers grapple with 'flying pigs' as food inflation soars

When it comes to buying food for daily meals, Chinese consumers are increasingly being forced to swallow unaffordable prices for a staple product — so-called flying pigs.

Supply-side problems have sent the price of pork surging this year, with the price trend becoming a fixture of local media reporting in the process.

Last month, pork prices rose by 85.7 per cent on-year and expanded 10.3 per cent from June, new data from the National Bureau of Statistics showed. The price of pork has more than doubled in the first seven months of the year from the same period in 2019.

(*Continued*)

(*Continued*)

Pork prices are rising because the stock of hogs and breeding sows are still recovering from the African Swine Fever epidemic that hit the country in late 2018, according to the government. The coronavirus pandemic and recent flooding in central and southern China have also hurt supply.

Meanwhile, demand for pork has risen quickly as more restaurants have resumed their business after nationwide coronavirus lockdowns early in the year.

Many Chinese consumers are starting to feel the pinch and some have been forced to cut back on purchases of the staple goods.

Source: Adapted from *South China Morning Post*, 10 Aug 2020. Retrieved on 19 August 2020 from: https://www.scmp.com/economy/china-economy/article/3096777/chinese-consumers-grapple-flying-pigs-and-rocketing-eggs

(a) With reference to Extract 1 and with the aid of a diagram, analyse the effects on the market for pork in China. [5]

Ans:
From Extract 1, the "supply-side problems" and restaurants resuming their business post-lockdowns are factors affecting the market for pork in China.

The "supply-side problems" refer to the slow recovery of hogs and breeding sows stocks, the coronavirus pandemic, and flooding in China. The latter two cause a fall in supply that outweighs the small increase in supply from the first factor. This causes an overall fall in the supply of pork. [1m]. At the same time, as restaurants resume their business, there would be an increase in demand for pork as people start eating out and consuming more pork as opposed to what they would consume at home. [1m]

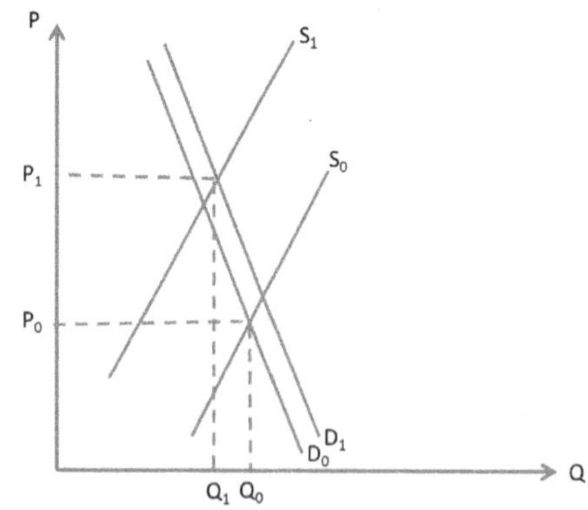

(*Continued*)

As shown in the diagram above [1m], as supply falls from S_0 to S_1 and demand increases from D_0 to D_1, a shortage is created, causing price to increase from P_0 to P_1. [1m] Whether the quantity traded increases or decreases depends on whether the decrease in supply outweighs the increase in demand. Assuming it does, the quantity traded would fall from Q_0 to Q_1. [1m]

Explanation of the answer:

- This question is like the one in worked example 3. The only differences are that the causes are no longer explicitly stated, and that there is a need to refer to Extract 1.
- Because the causes are not explicitly stated, we will need to find them from Extract 1. The answer is almost the same because the causes that we can find from Extract 1 are the same ones that were given in worked example 3. The only difference is that we now make it clear that the causes we found were from Extract 1 by writing "From Extract 1".

Note: This would have been a 6m question for H1 as the diagram would have been worth 2m since it had two curves shifting simultaneously.

Worked example 5

Extract 1: Chinese consumers grapple with 'flying pigs' as food inflation soars

When it comes to buying food for daily meals, Chinese consumers are increasingly being forced to swallow unaffordable prices for a staple product — so-called flying pigs.

Supply-side problems have sent the price of pork surging this year, with the price trend becoming a fixture of local media reporting in the process.

Last month, pork prices rose by 85.7 per cent on-year and expanded 10.3 per cent from June, new data from the National Bureau of Statistics showed. The price of pork has more than doubled in the first seven months of the year from the same period in 2019.

Pork prices are rising because the stock of hogs and breeding sows are still recovering from the African Swine Fever epidemic that hit the country

(*Continued*)

(*Continued*)

in late 2018, according to the government. The coronavirus pandemic and recent flooding in central and southern China have also hurt supply.

Meanwhile, demand for pork has risen quickly as more restaurants have resumed their business after nationwide coronavirus lockdowns early in the year.

Many Chinese consumers are starting to feel the pinch and some have been forced to cut back on purchases of the staple goods.

Source: Adapted from *South China Morning Post*, 10 Aug 2020. Retrieved on 19 August 2020 from: https://www.scmp.com/economy/china-economy/article/3096777/chinese-consumers-grapple-flying-pigs-and-rocketing-eggs

(a) With reference to Extract 1 and with the aid of a diagram, explain the increase in the price of pork. [4]

Ans:
From Extract 1, the "supply-side problems" and restaurants resuming their business post-lockdowns are factors affecting the market for pork in China.

The "supply-side problems" refer to the slow recovery of hogs and breeding sows stocks, the coronavirus pandemic, and flooding in China. The latter two cause a fall in supply that outweighs the small increase in supply from the first factor. This causes an overall fall in the supply of pork. [1m]. At the same time, as restaurants resume their business, there would be an increase in demand for pork as people start eating out and consuming more pork as opposed to what they would consume at home. [1m]

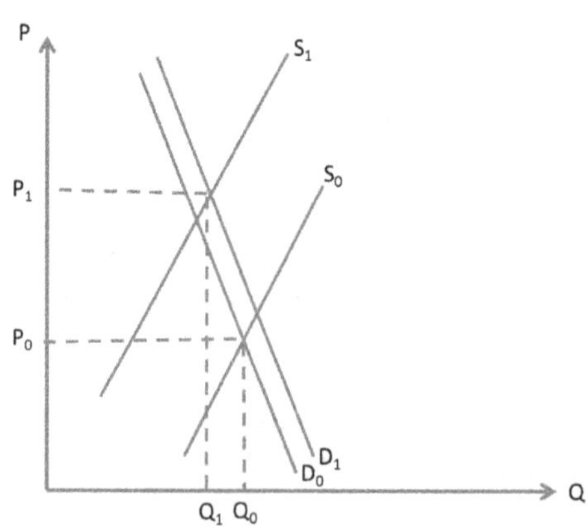

(*Continued*)

As shown in the diagram above [1m], as supply falls from S_0 to S_1 and demand increases from D_0 to D_1, a shortage is created, causing price to increase from P_0 to P_1. [1m]

Explanation of the answer:

- This question is like the one in worked example 4. The only differences are that the effect is "an increase in the price of food" instead of the effect on the market in general, and that there is a lower mark allocation. "Explain" and "analyse" are synonyms.
- Because the effect is now only an increase in the price of the food, step 4 would be:

"supply-side problems" → fall in supply overall → ↑ P (no need to explain change in Q)

restaurants resuming business → rise in demand ↗

(rise in demand: Demand and supply model)

The lower mark allocation is because there isn't a need to explain the change in quantity traded. So, in terms of details, there is a need to "zoom out" and provide fewer details.

Note: This would have been a 5m question for H1 as the diagram would have been worth 2m since it had two curves shifting simultaneously.

Worked example 6

Extract 1: Chinese consumers grapple with 'flying pigs' as food inflation soars

When it comes to buying food for daily meals, Chinese consumers are increasingly being forced to swallow unaffordable prices for a staple product — so-called flying pigs.

Supply-side problems have sent the price of pork surging this year, with the price trend becoming a fixture of local media reporting in the process.

Last month, pork prices rose by 85.7 per cent on-year and expanded 10.3 per cent from June, new data from the National Bureau of Statistics showed. The price of pork has more than doubled in the first seven months of the year from the same period in 2019.

(*Continued*)

(*Continued*)

Pork prices are rising because the stock of hogs and breeding sows are still recovering from the African Swine Fever epidemic that hit the country in late 2018, according to the government. The coronavirus pandemic and recent flooding in central and southern China have also hurt supply.

Meanwhile, demand for pork has risen quickly as more restaurants have resumed their business after nationwide coronavirus lockdowns early in the year.

Many Chinese consumers are starting to feel the pinch and some have been forced to cut back on purchases of the staple goods.

Source: Adapted from *South China Morning Post*, 10 Aug 2020. Retrieved on 19 August 2020 from: https://www.scmp.com/economy/china-economy/article/3096777/chinese-consumers-grapple-flying-pigs-and-rocketing-eggs

(a) With the aid of a diagram, explain how "supply-side problems" have "sent the price of pork surging". [5]

Ans:
The "supply-side problems" refer to the slow recovery of hogs and breeding sows stocks, the coronavirus pandemic, and flooding in China. The latter two cause a fall in supply that outweighs the small increase in supply from the first factor. This causes an overall fall in the supply of pork [1m]. As supply falls, a shortage is created, causing prices to increase from P0 to P1 [1m]. The extent of the rise in price would depend on the price elasticity of demand. As pork is a staple food in China (i.e., a necessity), the demand for pork is price inelastic [1m].

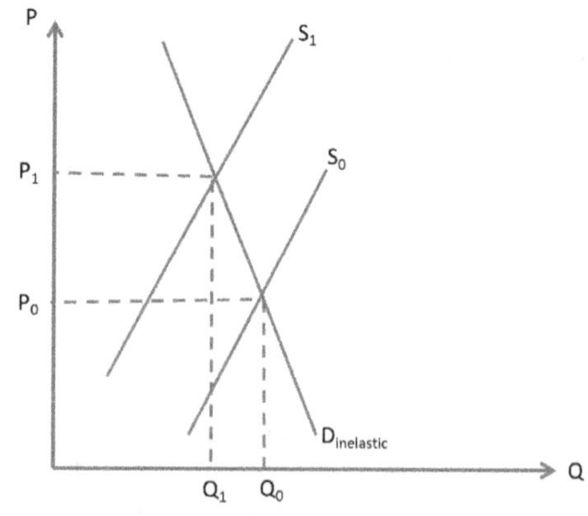

(*Continued*)

As such, as seen in the diagram above [1m], the fall in supply from S0 to S1 with a price inelastic demand would cause the price to increase more than proportionately (P0 to P1) compared to the fall in quantity (Q0 to Q1) [1m]. This large increase shows the price of pork "surging".

Explanation of the answer:

- This question is like the one in worked example 5. The differences are that there is only one cause ("supply-side problems") and that the effect is not just "an increase in price" but prices "surging".
- Since there is now only one cause, we drop the other cause from the explanation. This is straightforward.
- The change in effect (from simply an increase in price to a surge in price), however, makes a big difference. An increase in price only shows the direction of a change in price and hence demand and supply analysis is enough. "Surging" means that prices have not only increased. They have increased by a large extent. As such, we need to include the elasticity analysis (PED in this case)

Worked example 7

Extract 1: China exports rebound in April, but outlook remains grim

China's exports unexpectedly rose in April for the first time this year as factories raced to make up for lost sales due to the coronavirus shock, but a double-digit fall in imports signals more trouble ahead as the global economy sinks into recession.

Overseas shipments in April rose 3.5 per cent from a year earlier, marking the first positive growth since December last year, customs data showed on Thursday. The increase was driven in part by rising exports of medical equipment, traditional Chinese medicine and textiles, which include masks. China exported millions of tonnes of medical products worth 71.2 billion yuan (S$14.2 billion) in the March–April period, according to the customs agency. The daily export value of medical supplies jumped by more than three times last month.

In light of the rebound in April shipments, Nomura raised its forecasts for China's exports to minus 22 per cent for May and June from minus 30

(*Continued*)

(*Continued*)

per cent previously, but still deep in contraction as the coronavirus crisis ravages the global economy.

Source: *The Straits Times*, 7 May 2020. Retrieved on 15 May 2020 from: https://www.straitstimes.com/business/economy/china-exports-see-surprise-gain-in-april-but-rebound-seen-as-temporary

(a) With reference to Extract 1, explain how the "exports rebound" would affect China's economy. [4]

Ans:
The "exports rebound" refers to China's increase in export revenue (X) from medical equipment, traditional Chinese medicine and textiles. The rise in X would lead to an increase in aggregate demand (AD) as AD = consumption (C) + investments (I) + government spending (G) + net exports (X–M) [1m]. This would then cause firms' inventories to run down, leading to an increase in production in the next period. Increased output (economic growth) would simultaneously cause an increase in national income (NY) as more factor income would be paid out as firms increase output. Further, the increase in NY would be more than the increase in X due to the multiplier process. [1m] This rise in national output also implies a fall in unemployment as the increased production of goods and services would increase the demand for labour. [1m] In terms of inflation, since China was in a Covid-19-induced recession, there should be spare capacity in the economy and so the increase in AD would not create much inflationary pressure. [1m]

Explanation of the answer:

- Since the command word is "explain", this is an "explain" question and we can apply our steps.
- Step 1: Identify the cause and effect — In this case, the cause is "exports rebound" and the effect is the effect on "China's economy".
- Step 2: Unpack the effect in economic terms — Effect on an economy means the effect on the macroeconomic aims of growth, inflation, unemployment, and balance of trade (H2 only).
- Step 3: Determine the economic model to apply — Since the effect to be explained includes a change in NY (growth) and the GPL (inflation), the model to be used is the AD-AS model.

(*Continued*)

- Step 4: Link the cause to the model and then to the effect — In this case, we link the increase in X to an increase in AD and then to the various macroeconomic aims. Note that we need not always cover all the macroeconomic aims. We usually prioritise the effect on growth before seeing if there are marks "left over" to determine if we need to include the effects on the other aims. In this case, the link to growth does not warrant 4 marks and so we include some of the other macroeconomic aims.

5.8.4 *Common pitfalls to avoid*

For "explain" questions, once the question is analysed, the main problem faced is usually not an issue of skills but an issue of content. For example, even if a student knows that he/she needs to use the demand and supply model, if he/she does not know how the model works (e.g., does not know what factors shift demand or supply and the price adjustment process), then he/she would still be unable to answer the question.

5.9 How to Answer a "Discuss" (or a Synonym) Question

A "discuss" question has the command word "discuss". There are also other ways to phrase a define question that are shown in Table 5.27.

Although the command words are different, all the questions are asking for the exact same thing.

5.9.1 *Mark allocation*

"Discuss" questions are different from all the previous case study questions that we have looked at so far. "Discuss" questions are considered higher-order thinking questions and are thus marked by levels

Table 5.27: Command words which are synonymous with "discuss".

Command Word/Phrase	Sample Question
Discuss...	In light of the case material presented, discuss whether globalisation is a "force for good".
Assess...	In light of the case material presented, assess whether globalisation is a "force for good".
Evaluate...	In light of the case material presented, evaluate whether globalisation is a "force for good".
Comment...	In light of the case material presented, comment on whether globalisation is a "force for good".

Table 5.28: Mark allocation for "discuss" questions.

For a 8m "Discuss" question	For a 10m "Discuss" Question
Level 2 [4–6 marks]	Level 2 [5–7 marks]
Level 1 [1–3 marks]	Level 1 [1–4 marks]
Evaluation [1–2 marks]	Evaluation [1–3 marks]

rather than by points. Each level would have a set of descriptors and the answer would be read as a whole and placed in a level based on which descriptor it best matches. Separately, marks are reserved for evaluative conclusions/comments. So, an answer would be assigned level marks and evaluation to get the total marks for that question (e.g., L2 – 5 marks and Ev – 1 mark to get 6 marks in total). The mark breakdown is shown in Table 5.28.

For H1 Economics, there is an additional 6-mark "discuss" question that typically has "comment" as the command word. This is the exception as it is not usually marked purely by levels. Instead, there are typically 4 marks for an explanation (that is marked by points) and then a further 2 marks for some evaluative comment on the explanation provided. See section 5.10.1 below for details of how to answer it. A separate section has been written for it as the skills for answering the 8-mark and 10-mark "discuss" questions are similar for H1 and H2 and are covered together in this section.

While the specific descriptors for the levels would vary from question to question, the descriptors for the highest level often contain the following elements:

- **Balance** — This refers to having both a thesis and an anti-thesis. For instance, if the question is "Discuss whether the Federal Reserve should raise interest rates", then the thesis would be "The Federal Reserve should raise interest rates" and the anti-thesis would be "The Federal Reserve should not raise interest rates". An answer would only be balanced if it includes points for both the thesis and the anti-thesis.
- **Context** — This refers to inclusion of points relevant to the context given in the case material. This is usually shown by making references to the case material.
- **Depth** — This refers to the use of economic analysis in the explanations. It usually involves using an economic model and reference to graphs.

To illustrate balance, context, and depth more concretely, we will look at a few positive and negative examples to the question: "Discuss whether the Federal Reserve should raise interest rates".

The answer in the left column of Table 5.29 shows balance as it has a point supporting the thesis ("Federal Reserve should raise interest rates") and a point supporting the anti-thesis ("Federal Reserve should not raise interest rates"). In contrast, the answer in the right column explains only points that support the thesis and as such, is not balanced.

Do note that balance does not mean that there must be an equal number of thesis and anti-thesis points. Such thinking tends to lead to forced arguments. Instead, as long as there is at least one point on each side, the answer is considered balanced.

The paragraph in the left column of Table 5.30 shows the use of context as it shows that US may have inflationary pressures, which makes

Table 5.29: Contrasting a balanced answer with one that is not.

A Balanced Answer	A One-Sided Answer
The Federal Reserve ought to raise interest rates to stave off possible inflation. Extract 1 points to the US labour market tightening, which would place upward pressure on wages. This would translate into an increase in the cost of production and hence inflationary pressure as firms pass on higher costs as higher prices. Raising interest rates would help to prevent this problem by causing the costs of borrowing to increase and hence reduce purchase of big-ticket items as well as investments. Both the reduction in consumption and investments would lead to a fall in AD, which would then cause the GPL to decrease. This would, in turn, offset inflationary pressures.	The Federal Reserve ought to raise interest rates to stave off possible inflation. Extract 1 points to the US labour market tightening, which would place upward pressure on wages. This would translate into an increase in the cost of production and hence inflationary pressure as firms pass on higher costs as higher prices. Raising interest rates would help to prevent this problem by causing the costs of borrowing to increase and hence reduce purchase of big-ticket items as well as investments. Both the reduction in consumption and investments would lead to a fall in AD, which would then cause the GPL to decrease. This would, in turn, offset inflationary pressures.
However, a counter-argument is that the economy is only experiencing "tepid recovery" (Extract 2). This means that real GDP is only increasing to a small extent. As such, the reduction in national output from the fall in AD due to the increase in interest rates explained earlier might push the economy back into a recession.	Furthermore, interest rates in the US has been close to zero. Assuming interest rates cannot go below zero, the current rates leave little room for expansionary monetary policy if required. Raising rates would thus be beneficial in terms of creating space for an expansionary monetary policy if required in the future.

the raising of interest rates appropriate. Explicit references are highlighted to make the cue words that show context more visible. In contrast, the paragraph in the right column is theoretical. It explains how raising interest rates works in theory to control inflation but does not show application to the context as it does not show evidence from the case material that US is facing inflationary pressures.

Do note that not every single point/paragraph needs to include explicit reference to the case material. Instead, across the entire

Table 5.30: Contrasting a paragraph that uses context with one that does not.

A Paragraph that Uses the Context	A Purely Theoretical Paragraph
The Federal reserve ought to raise interest rates to stave off possible inflation. Extract 1 points to the US labour market tightening, which would place upward pressure on wages. This would translate into an increase in the cost of production and hence inflationary pressure as firms pass on higher costs as higher prices. Raising interest rates would help to prevent this problem by causing the costs of borrowing to increase and hence reduce purchase of big-ticket items as well as investments. Both the reduction in consumption and investments would lead to a fall in AD, which would then cause the GPL to decrease. This would, in turn, offset inflationary pressures.	The Federal should raise interest rates because it is a contractionary monetary policy that can control inflation. An increase in interest rates causes the costs of borrowing to increase. As such, consumers will reduce purchase of big-ticket items and firms will cut back on investments. Both the reduction in consumption and investments would lead to a fall in AD, which would then cause the GPL to decrease. This prevents demand-pull inflation.

answer, there should be some references so that the entire answer is not purely theoretical. Also, reference to the case material need not involve quoting sentences directly. Paraphrasing or summarising the case material is fine as long as the source is quoted (i.e., instead of writing "Extract 1 states that 'the tightening of the labour market is one of these indicators, with job creation at the highest since 2008'", it is alright to summarise and write "Extract 1 points to the US labour market tightening").

The difference between the paragraphs with great/some depth and the paragraph with no depth is the use of economic models (Table 5.31). In this case, the economic model required was the AD–AS model (highlighted). The paragraph with no depth did not use any economic model. The purpose of contrasting a paragraph with great depth and a paragraph with some depth is to show that the depth of the explanation is on a continuum. The more details provided (i.e., the more "zoomed in" the explanation is), the greater the depth.

Table 5.31: Contrasting a paragraph with depth against a shallow paragraph.

A Paragraph with Great Depth	**A Paragraph with Some Depth**	**A Paragraph with No Depth**
The Federal reserve ought to raise interest rates to stave off possible inflation. Extract 1 points to the US labour market tightening, which would place upward pressure on wages. This would translate into an increase in the cost of production and hence inflationary pressure as firms pass on higher costs as higher prices. Raising interest rates would help to prevent this problem by causing the costs of borrowing to increase and hence reduce purchase of big-ticket items as well as investments. Both the reduction in consumption and investments would lead to a fall in AD. 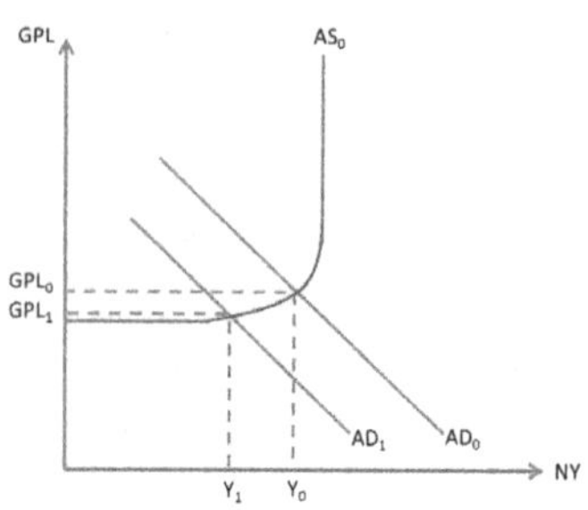 As seen in the diagram above, the fall in AD from AD_0 to AD_1 would then cause the GPL to decrease from GPL_0 to GPL_1, which will in turn offset inflationary pressures.	The Federal reserve ought to raise interest rates to stave off possible inflation. Extract 1 points to the US labour market tightening, which would eventually lead to higher inflation. Raising interest rates would help to prevent this problem by causing the costs of borrowing to increase and hence reduce purchase of big-ticket items as well as investments. Both the reduction in consumption and investments would lead to a fall in AD, which would then cause the GPL to decrease. This would in turn, offset inflationary pressures.	The Federal reserve ought to raise interest rates to stave off possible inflation. Extract 1 points to the US labour market tightening, which would eventually lead to higher inflation. Raising interest rates would makes people buy less goods and hence bring down inflation.

Note that not every point in the answer must have great depth. In fact, there may even be some points in the answer that do not require an economic model (but these should not be many). How much depth to provide is also a matter of the mark allocation and the number of points to cover. Nonetheless, most of the time, the explanation of a point will require the application of an economic model.

5.9.2 *How to answer it*

Most "discuss" questions require a four-part answer — an introduction, a thesis, an anti-thesis, and an evaluative conclusion (or a synthesis). Note that this does not mean that every answer to a "discuss" question would have four paragraphs since there could be multiple points (and hence multiple paragraphs) for the thesis and/or for the anti-thesis. There are some exceptions where there is no clear thesis and anti-thesis and we will consider such cases in the box at the end of this section. For a start, we will focus on the typical "discuss" question that requires a thesis and anti-thesis. It is important to first plan for the answer before writing it. And, to draw up a plan, you would need to analyse the question using the 3C+ framework introduced at the start of Chapter 5.

Based on the 3C+ question analysis, we then do our planning where we (i) develop the thesis and anti-thesis statements, (ii) select the relevant points for inclusion, and (iii) plan the evaluation. Only after the planning do we write the answer out in full (i.e., point development).

Let us see what is involved in each of these.

Step 1: (Planning) Develop the thesis and anti-thesis statements
Since most "discuss" questions require explanations of both the thesis and anti-thesis, the first step is to determine what the thesis and anti-thesis statements are. To do this, when you do your 3C+ question analysis, try to focus on the content that the command word is

applied to and generate two sides for it. Let's take a look at some examples.

Example 1: "In light of the features of the US shale oil industry, discuss whether the US government should intervene in the domestic shale oil market."

Applying the 3C+ question analysis, we see that the:

- Command word = "discuss". This tells us that we would need to develop a thesis and anti-thesis, and that we would need to write a synthesis (i.e., evaluative conclusion) at the end.
- Content = "whether the US government should intervene in the domestic shale oil market". Recall that the content is the thing that we are supposed to apply the command word to. In this case, what we are supposed to discuss is whether the US government should intervene.
- Context = US's shale oil market.
- Additional conditions (+) = "In light of the features of the US shale oil industry".

The content is what we look at to generate the thesis and anti-thesis. We try to generate two sides to the content. In this case, given that the content is whether the US government should intervene, the thesis would be "the US government should intervene in the domestic shale oil market" while the anti-thesis would be "the US government should not intervene in the domestic shale oil market".

At this point, you might wonder about the purpose of the context and additional conditions. They will be helpful in the point selection that we will cover later.

Example 2: "Assess the policies that the Australian government has adopted in response to the "unprecedented disruption to global trade" (Extract 3)."

Applying the 3C+ question analysis, we see that the:

- Command word = "Assess". This is a synonym of "discuss" and hence also requires a thesis, anti-thesis, and synthesis.
- Content = "policies that the Australian government has adopted…". The thing to be assessed is the policies that the Australian government has adopted.
- Context = Australia.
- Additional conditions (+) = Nil.

In Example 2, since the content to be assessed are the policies that the Australian government has adopted, we need to generate a thesis and anti-thesis for it. So, the thesis could be that "the policies adopted by the Australian government are appropriate/effective" and the anti-thesis would be that "the policies adopted by the Australian government are inappropriate/ineffective".

A good tip when you are stuck and cannot think of a thesis and anti-thesis is to think broadly in terms of good vs bad. Like in this case, we knew we needed two sides to the policies so we went with "policies good" vs "policies bad" and that allowed us to develop a thesis and an anti-thesis.

Example 3: "Evaluate the effects of "3D printing… becoming an increasingly viable alternative means of production" (Extract 2) on small and open economies like Singapore."

Applying the 3C+ question analysis, we see that the:

- Command word = "Evaluate". This is a synonym of "discuss" and hence also requires a thesis, anti-thesis, and synthesis.
- Content = "effects… on small and open economies like Singapore". The thing to be evaluated is the effect of 3D printing becoming more viable on small and open economies like Singapore.
- Context = small and open economies like Singapore.
- Additional conditions (+) = Nil.

In Example 3, since the content to be evaluated are the effects on small and open economies, we generate the thesis and anti-thesis for it. Using the tip of good vs bad, we can think of "good effects" vs "bad effects". So, the thesis would be "3D printing becoming an increasingly viable alternative means of production would have beneficial effects on small and open economies like Singapore" while the anti-thesis would be "3D printing becoming an increasingly viable alternative means of production would have harmful effects on small and open economies like Singapore".

Note that there may be more than one way to generate the thesis and anti-thesis. An equally acceptable set of thesis and anti-thesis could be "3D printing becoming an increasingly viable alternative means of production would have large effects on small and open economies like Singapore" vs "3D printing becoming an increasingly viable alternative means of production would have small effects on small and open economies like Singapore".

Having said that, you will find that often, your thesis and anti-thesis being constructed along the lines of good vs bad make for easier point development later.

Example 4: "With reference to the relevant case material, comment on the future prices of sweet potatoes".

Applying the 3C+ question analysis, we see that the:

- Command word = "Comment on". This is a synonym of "discuss" and hence also requires a thesis, anti-thesis, and synthesis.
- Content = "the future prices of sweet potatoes". The thing to be commented on is the future prices of sweet potatoes.
- Context = sweet potato market.
- Additional conditions (+) = "With reference to the relevant case material".

In Example 4, since the content to be commented on is the future prices of sweet potatoes, we generate the thesis and anti-thesis for it.

For this example, clearly the good vs bad tip does not help ("future price good" vs "future price bad" does not make much sense). Instead, since price is just a value/number, the thesis could be "future price would increase" and the anti-thesis could be "future price would decrease".

This gives us another tip — that if we are asked to discuss a value (e.g., price, output, revenue, GDP), the thesis and anti-thesis could be along the lines of increase vs decrease.

The four examples above show us how to generate a thesis and anti-thesis when we need to answer a "discuss" question. At the stage of generating the thesis and anti-thesis, it is possible that you may realise that there is no plausible thesis and anti-thesis. For example, if you need to discuss the factors that an economic agent should consider when making decisions, you may not be able to generate a thesis and anti-thesis. Such instances are unusual and we will deal with them in the box at the end of this segment.

Developing the thesis and anti-thesis when you plan for your answer will ensure that when you write your answer, it will always meet the marking criteria of being balanced.

Step 2: (Planning) Select the relevant points

After you have developed the thesis and anti-thesis, you need to select points to include to support the thesis and the anti-thesis. There are two ways to do this — (i) select the points from the case material as if you were doing an English comprehension passage and (ii) generate theoretical points. If the first approach allows you to generate sufficient points, then there is no need to for the latter. However, you must always be prepared to do (ii) as it is possible that the case material does not provide sufficient points (e.g., it only provides points for the thesis but not the anti-thesis) or that the question is more theoretical in nature (e.g., if it requires you to discuss possible policies that a government could adopt).

Furthermore, whether you are selecting the points from the case material or using theoretical points, the points must be relevant to the context and satisfy the additional requirements. For example, if the question were "In light of the features of the US shale oil industry, discuss whether the US government should intervene in the domestic shale oil market", the context would be the US shale oil market and the additional conditions that we must take note of are the features of the US shale oil industry. As such, the points that are used must be applicable to the US shale oil industry and be related to the features of the industry. So, points such as "the US government should intervene in the industry to improve macroeconomic performance by exporting the oil" would not be relevant since it is not related to the features of the industry (features of the industry here presumably refers to the characteristics of the market such as the level of competition that exists in the market).

In terms of the number of points needed, you will need two points minimally (one for the thesis and one for the anti-thesis). Whether you should include three points (one for the thesis and two for the anti-thesis or the other way around) or more depends on the mark allocation. A rule of thumb would be to provide two points for questions that carry up to 8 marks and at least three points for questions carrying more than 8 marks.

We will see how this is done in the worked examples later.

Step 3: (Planning) Plan the evaluation

There is considerable confusion over what counts as an evaluation. A common misconception is that to gain evaluation marks, one must bring in information that is outside of the scope of the question. This belief causes students to memorise "evaluation points" that they can regurgitate in examinations. This is misguided. New information may be completely irrelevant to answering the question. For example, if you were asked whether Singapore should tighten foreign labour inflow, and you provided little known details of how exactly Singapore implements the basket, band, and crawl system in our exchange rate policy, you would have provided rich real world knowledge that adds nothing to answering the question and so would not be rewarded (except, perhaps, one mark out of pity).

What then, is evaluation about? The Singapore Examination and Assessment Board's (SEAB) syllabus documents[4] note that for evaluation, students are expected to:

- Evaluate critically, contemporary issues, perspectives and policy choices.
- Recognise unstated assumptions and evaluate their relevance.
- Synthesise economic arguments to arrive at well-reasoned judgements and decisions.

Of the three, the third bullet point is the focus of this section as it lends itself best to conclusions, which will always be required. In contrast, while the other two approaches could contribute to earning some evaluation marks, they may not always be applicable. We will still cover them briefly when we look at how to answer "discuss" questions with no clear thesis or anti-thesis later. For now, however, we will focus on writing evaluative conclusions that synthesise arguments.

To synthesise the thesis and anti-thesis, we should bear in mind two "J"s — judgement and justification.

First, we must recognise the possible judgements we can make in answering the question. These judgements can generally go in three directions — overall support for the thesis, overall support for the anti-thesis, or not being able to make a judgement (yes, "I don't know" is a judgement too. It is usually wise to admit ignorance rather than cook up a judgement that you are not convinced by.). Note that these judgements must answer the question and in weighing the thesis against the anti-thesis, we would naturally do so. Table 5.32 shows examples of possible judgements to the "discuss" questions we used earlier as examples.

To come to the judgement, we need to go through a logical process of weighing the thesis against the anti-thesis. This gives us the other

Table 5.32: Possible evaluative judgements to write in conclusions.

Question	Thesis vs Anti-Thesis	Possible Evaluative Judgements
In light of the features of the US shale oil industry, discuss whether the US government should intervene in the domestic shale oil market.	• Thesis: the US government should intervene in the domestic shale oil market. • Anti-thesis: the US government should not intervene in the domestic shale oil market.	• Overall, the US government should intervene in the domestic shale oil market. • Overall, the US government should not intervene in the domestic shale oil market. • It is not possible to make a judgement about whether on balance, the US government should intervene without more information.
Assess the policies that the Australian government has adopted in response to the "unprecedented disruption to global trade" (Extract 3).	• Thesis: the policies adopted by the Australian government are appropriate/effective. • Anti-thesis: the policies adopted by the Australian government are inappropriate/ineffective.	• Overall, the policies adopted by the Australian government are appropriate/effective. • Overall, the policies adopted by the Australian government are inappropriate/ineffective. • It is not possible to make a judgement about whether the policies adopted by the Australian government were inappropriate/ineffective overall without more information.

Table 5.32: (*Continued*)

Question	Thesis vs Anti-Thesis	Possible Evaluative Judgements
Evaluate the effects of "3D printing... becoming an increasingly viable alternative means of production" (Extract 2) on small and open economies like Singapore.	• Thesis: "3D printing becoming an increasingly viable alternative means of production would have beneficial effects on small and open economies like Singapore". • Anti-thesis: "3D printing becoming an increasingly viable alternative means of production would have harmful effects on small and open economies like Singapore".	• Overall, 3D printing becoming an increasingly viable alternative means of production would have beneficial effects on small and open economies like Singapore. • Overall, 3D printing becoming an increasingly viable alternative means of production would have harmful effects on small and open economies like Singapore. • It is not possible to make a judgement about the net effects of 3D printing on the Singapore economy without more information.
With reference to the relevant case material, comment on the future prices of sweet potatoes".	• Thesis: future price would increase. • Anti-thesis: future price would decrease.	• Overall, the future price of sweet potatoes would increase. • Overall, the future price of sweet potatoes would decrease. • It is not possible to make a judgement about whether the price of sweet potatoes would increase or decrease without more information.

"J" — justification. For the justification, it is always good to acknowledge that the context determines whether the thesis outweighs the anti-thesis. For example, if the question is whether the Singapore government should implement minimum wages, then the points supporting the thesis might be that minimum wages would reduce income inequality by lifting incomes at the bottom while the antithesis could be that such a policy might increase the cost of living by increasing the cost of production. Whether a minimum wage creates net benefits would then depend on the extent of these benefits and costs, which would in turn depend on the context of Singapore. For example, knowing that Singapore does not specialise in producing low value-added and labour-intensive goods would allow us to argue that the increase in cost of production from having a minimum wage would be limited since the portion of cost spent on low-wage labour is small to begin with. As such, you can reach the judgement that Singapore should implement minimum wages since the costs of it are low and the benefits would outweigh the cost. Note that the questions do not usually require you to make a judgement in a specific direction. Rather, you are being graded for whether your argument is coherent. So, as long as you make sense in reaching your judgement, you will earn the evaluation marks.

Typical aspects of the context that can help us determine the extent of effects could be:

- **Time** — Some effects dominate in the short run while others dominate in the long run. You can then make a conclusion about the short run and the long run separately.
- **State of a country** — Whether some factors are more important than others may depend on the state of the country. For example, if people in a country have high incomes but are constantly stressed and unhappy, income would be a less important factor than stress levels in determining the standard of living. Or, if a country is operating close to full capacity, then the risk of inflation is greater than the risk of unemployment.
- **Whether the government is able to mitigate some factors** — If a government is able to mitigate some of the factors, then those factors are less important (e.g., a minimum wage to reduce income

inequality is less pressing if there are already other policies like the Workfare Income Supplement to reduce income inequality).

Plan for the evaluation by working through a justification to reach a judgement. More details on how to write a justified judgement will be provided in Section 5.10 as well as in the worked examples.

Step 4: Write out your answer in full

- **Writing the introduction** — you will notice that at the planning stage, we did not plan for an introduction. This is because introductions are straightforward to write. Define terms and set the stage for your answer by introducing your thesis and anti-thesis. Sometimes, some background explanation may also be required. For example, if you were asked to discuss policies, you should first clarify what problem the policies are supposed to solve.
- **Writing the body** — write each point in the body as a fresh paragraph. This makes each point more salient. For each point's development, write it as if you were answering an "explain" question. For example, if the point to be made is that "the price of sweet potatoes will rise in the future", write it as if you were answering the question "Explain why the price of sweet potatoes will rise in the future". This means to start at the cause, make a link to an economic model (where applicable), and then make a link to the effect. Refer to Section 5.7 for the details on how to answer an "explain" question.
- **Writing the evaluative conclusion** — We already know that in the conclusion, we want to make a judgement that answers the question and justify this judgement by synthesising the thesis and anti-thesis. A useful guide is to follow these steps:
  - Show that the judgement depends on weighing the thesis against the anti-thesis points.
  - Show that the context determines whether the thesis outweighs the anti-thesis.
  - Make a judgement based on the context.

A sample template would be:

> "In conclusion, (the judgement to be made) would depend on the relative importance of (thesis and anti-thesis points). Given (insert the context), (the thesis points) would outweigh/be outweighed by (the anti-thesis points). As such, (make the judgement)."

For example, suppose the question is "Discuss whether the Singapore government should implement minimum wages" and that the thesis point is that minimum wages would reduce income inequality by lifting incomes at the bottom while the anti-thesis point is that such a policy might increase the cost of living by increasing the cost of production. Following the template, the conclusion could be (the parts that were filled in are underlined):

> "In conclusion, <u>whether Singapore should implement a minimum wage</u> would depend on the relative importance of <u>reducing income inequality</u> and <u>the increasing cost of living</u>. Given <u>Singapore's context where there are already existing policies such as the progressive wage model as well as the workfare income supplement to reduce the income inequality, the need to implement new policies to reduce income inequality is less pressing</u> and hence would be outweighed by <u>the need to the prevent costs of living from rising</u>. As such, <u>Singapore should not implement a minimum wage</u>."

Note that an opposite conclusion like the one below is also equally valid. What matters is making sure your thought process is clearly explained and not so much what conclusion you reach.

> "In conclusion, <u>whether Singapore should implement a minimum wage</u> would depend on the relative importance of <u>reducing income inequality</u> and <u>the increasing cost of living</u>. Given <u>Singapore's context where the income inequality has increased significantly despite the existing measures while inflation (and hence costs of living) remains at only about 1–2% a year</u>, <u>the need to stem the rise in further income</u>

> inequality would outweigh the need to the prevent costs of living from rising. As such, Singapore should implement a minimum wage."

For the examples above, we used the context of whether the government is able to mitigate some factors and the state of the country to make the judgement. The worked examples in the next section will show how the time period could be used as a context to make the judgement.

At this point, you will likely have two further questions — what if you do not have information about the context given (e.g., you did not know about the progressive wage model), and what if the question does not specify a context? Let's look at each one in turn.

If you do not have information about a given context — After writing that the judgement depends on the relative importance of the thesis and anti-thesis points, and that the context will determine whether the thesis outweighs the anti-thesis, explain what information/data you would need and how you would use this information/data to make a judgement. See the example below (imagine you knew nothing of Singapore's context):

> "In conclusion, whether Singapore should implement a minimum wage would depend on the relative importance of reducing income inequality and the increasing cost of living. This would depend on the context and we would need to collect information on the extent of income inequality (e.g., the Gini coefficient) as well as information on the cost of living (e.g., the inflation rate) to make the judgement. If the Gini coefficient is very high while inflation is low, then income inequality is a more pressing concern than the costs of living and a minimum wage should be implemented. Conversely, if the Gini coefficient is not very high while the inflation rate is high, then a minimum wage should not be implemented."

If the question does not specify a context — It is quite unlikely that a case study question would not have a specific context specified. However, if it does happen (e.g., if the question is not "Discuss whether the Singapore government should implement minimum wages" but "Discuss whether governments should implement minimum wages"), the approach would still be similar. The only difference would be that you could bring in a specific country's context as an example:

> "In conclusion, whether any government should implement a minimum wage would depend on the relative importance of reducing income inequality and preventing an increase in the cost of living in that country. This would depend on the country's specific context. For example, Singapore's income inequality has increased significantly while its inflation (and hence cost of living) remains at only about 1–2% a year. As such, for Singapore, the need to stem the rise in further income inequality would outweigh the need to the prevent the cost of living from rising. As such, Singapore should implement a minimum wage."

5.9.3 *Worked examples*

In this section, we will provide just one worked example because of the length of case material required (this book is getting a little too long as it is).

Worked example

Extract 1: China needs to weigh economic 'consequences' of coronavirus stimulus, top Beijing researcher says

China needs to consider the costs of its emergency coronavirus stimulus and prepare to scale back support in a timely manner, according to a top researcher in Beijing.

China has released a flurry of stimulus measures to revive the economy in recent months, including tax exemptions and lifting the fiscal deficit ratio to 3.6 per cent of gross domestic product (GDP). The People's Bank of China (PBOC) has also cut the required reserve ratio three times this year, freeing up 1.75 trillion yuan (US$250 billion) into the banking system by reducing the amount of money that banks are required to hold in reserve. This effectively increases the money supply.

(*Continued*)

But Gao Peiyong, vice-president at Chinese Academy of Social Sciences, a think tank affiliated with the State Council, told an online forum at the weekend that China had not paid enough attention to the side effects of the package aimed at stabilising growth and jobs, both of which have been hammered by the Covid-19 pandemic.

"Relating to macroeconomic policy, attention hasn't been paid to the costs," Gao said, according to a transcript published by news website Sina. com. "It is necessary for us to fully evaluate such consequences and possible negative effects, and be prepared to exit the expansionary macroeconomic policy in a timely manner.

"Whether it is fiscal policy or monetary policy, I think it is necessary to consider."

Gao warned about the risks of a record high fiscal deficit and growing debt among cash-strapped local governments.

Additionally, there are concerns with excess liquidity from loose monetary policy fuelling spending in stocks and real estate, leading to dangerous asset bubbles in the stock market and the property market.

Source: Adapted from *South China Morning Post*, 27 July 2020. Retrieved on 19 Aug 2020 from: https://www.scmp.com/economy/article/3094811/china-needs-weigh-economic-consequences-coronavirus-stimulus-top-beijing

Question: In light of the Covid-19 pandemic, discuss the desirability of China's macroeconomic policy stance. [10]

Stage 1: Question analysis

- Command word = "discuss". This is a "discuss" question which will require a thesis, anti-thesis, and a synthesis for the conclusion.
- Content = "the desirability of China's macroeconomic policy stance". This is the thing to be discussed. From here, we can get the thesis and anti-thesis:
  - Thesis: China's macroeconomic policy stance is desirable.
  - Anti-thesis: China's macroeconomic policy stance is undesirable.
- Context = China. The points used must be relevant to China.
- Additional conditions (+) = "In light of the Covid-19 pandemic". So, whether the policy stance is desirable would need to take into account the problems caused by the Covid-19 pandemic.

(*Continued*)

(*Continued*)

Stage 2: Planning

- Select the points for the thesis and anti-thesis from the case material as well as from the relevant theory:

Thesis: China's macroeconomic policy stance is desirable	Anti-thesis: China's macroeconomic policy stance is undesirable
• Covid-19 pandemic has caused the economy to contract ("hammered by the Covid-19 pandemic"). China's expansionary policy stance (both monetary and fiscal policy) would help to correct the reduction in real GDP and reduce unemployment.	(From the last two paragraph) • Expansionary fiscal policy may lead to debt problems for cash-strapped local governments. • Extended expansionary monetary policy might lead to asset price inflation (e.g., property price inflation).
Evaluation: Judgement must be about whether China's macroeconomic policy stance is desirable. This will depend on whether the thesis outweighs the anti-thesis (need to use China's context to determine this).	

Note that because this is a 10m question, we will use all the points in the plan above. If it were an 8m question, two well-explained points in the body (i.e., one point for the thesis and one for the anti-thesis) would be sufficient.

Stage 3: Writing out the full answer (notice how (1) the background of how the Covid-19 pandemic would shrink the economy is briefly explained in the introduction, (2) each point in the body uses economic analysis and (3) how the conclusion is structured to reach a justified judgement)

Introduction

The Covid-19 pandemic would cause a shrinkage of the Chinese economy as public health measures to get people to stay home and not socialise would cause a reduction in consumption (C). This would also dampen business confidence and cause a fall in investments (I). The fall in C and I would cause aggregate demand (AD) to fall and hence cause national output to decline, pushing China into a recession. Further, the fall in national output would also create unemployment as firms' demand for labour would fall when they reduce production. China's macroeconomic policy stance is expansionary and

(*Continued*)

its desirability would depend on how well it addresses the problems caused by the pandemic as well as whether it creates other negative side effects.

Body 1: Thesis — Explain how China's expansionary policy stance (both fiscal and monetary) would correct the contraction from the pandemic

China's fiscal policy is an expansionary one as it has introduced tax exemptions and increased the fiscal deficit (Extract 1), which we can interpret as a reduction in taxes and an increase in government spending (G). A reduction in personal income tax would lead to higher post-tax disposable incomes and hence stimulate consumption (C) as purchasing power increases. For firms, a reduction in corporate income tax would raise post-tax profits and make more investment projects appear profitable. This would stimulate investment (I). Taken together, the fiscal policy would lead to an increase in aggregate demand (AD) through increasing C, I, and G since AD = C + I + G (government expenditure) + X–M (net exports).

China's monetary policy is also expansionary since lowering the required reserve ratio "effectively increases the money supply" (Extract 1). Since money supply and interest rates have an inverse relationship, an increased money supply pushes down the interest rates. This further stimulates C and I as lower interest rates translate into lower costs of borrowing, which makes the consumption of big-ticket items on credit cheaper and also makes more investment projects profitable. Coupled with the expansionary fiscal policy explained earlier, the overall effect of China's macroeconomic policy stance is an increase in AD.

This is desirable as helps to prevent the recession and unemployment caused by the pandemic.

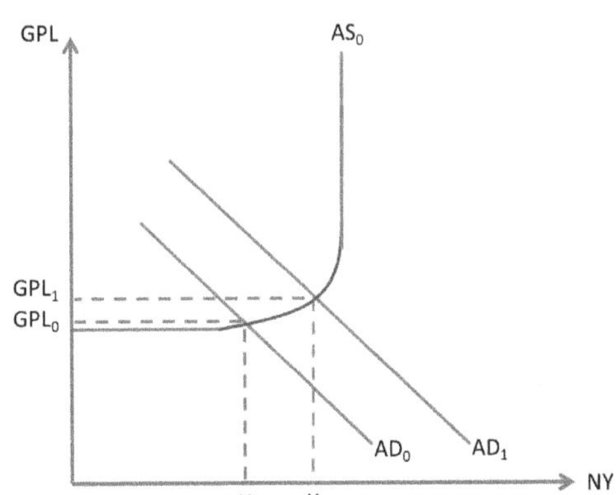

(*Continued*)

(*Continued*)

From the diagram above, the increase in AD from AD_0 to AD_1 would cause firms' inventories to run down and hence stimulate more production in the next period. This increases national output from Y_0 to Y_1. Further, because of the multiplier process, the increase in NY would be a multiple of the original increase in AD. The increase in national output would also lower unemployment as firms would demand more factors of production (including labour) to produce the additional output, creating jobs in the process. These correct the problems caused by the pandemic (Extract states that "growth and jobs... have been hammered by the Covid-19 pandemic"). Hence, China's macroeconomic policy stance is desirable.

<u>Body 2: Anti-thesis — Explain how China's macroeconomic policy stance would create negative side-effects such as debt problems for cash-strapped local governments</u>

However, an overly expansionary fiscal policy may not be as desirable if it leads to negative side effects such as debt problems for cash-strapped local governments. If local governments of Chinese counties do not have enough reserves, the expansionary fiscal policy must be funded by government borrowing. This causes local governments to accumulate government debt. This may not be desirable as higher debt also means higher future interest payments to service the debt (*note*: debt servicing refers to paying the interest payments on the debt). This imposes an opportunity cost as future local government revenue will have to be used for debt servicing and benefits from alternative spending such as benefits from education or healthcare spending would have to be foregone.

<u>Body 3: Anti-thesis — Explain how China's macroeconomic policy stance would create negative side-effects such as asset inflation</u>

Additionally, the expansionary monetary policy may not be desirable as it could lead to "dangerous asset bubbles". Low interest rates not only represent lower costs of borrowing but also lower returns on savings. As such, investors/savers would turn towards alternative assets such as stocks or property to try to get a better return (e.g., through rental or selling the property at a higher price if the price rises). This would drive up the demand for such assets and hence increase their prices. This could then form a bubble if it becomes a self-fulfilling prophecy where investors

(*Continued*)

expect prices to increase and so demand more of the asset, which further drives the prices up. A bubble is dangerous because once there is a trigger for the price to fall, all the speculators would dump the asset and the price will crash. People who bought the asset at a high price would then lose all their money. Because of such a possible side-effect, an overly expansionary monetary policy may not be desirable.

Evaluative conclusion

In conclusion, whether China's macroeconomic policy response is desirable would depend on whether the gains from countering the effects of the pandemic outweighs the cost of the side-effects of accumulating government debt and asset price inflation. This depend on the time period. In the short run, given the large scale of the pandemic, it is more important to mitigate its worst effects. As such, the policy is desirable. In the longer term however, the effects of the pandemic should weaken as vaccines are developed and distributed while the risk of accumulated debt and asset bubbles would increase. Hence, it may not be desirable to maintain the expansionary stance in the long run.

5.9.4 *Common pitfalls to avoid*

For "discuss" questions in a case study, once students understand how to analyse the question, achieving balance and scope are often not difficult. The differentiating factor is usually depth. Most answers use similar points but score differently because of a difference in the amount of economic analysis employed. As such, a common pitfall to avoid is to avoid answering the question as if it were a simple comprehension question. Inclusion of graphs (as well as describing them) would ensure that the problem is avoided.

A related problem is that students sometimes sacrifice depth for scope by trying to include many points but only explaining each point briefly. This results in a poorer answer than one with fewer but more completely explained points. It is good to remember that not every possible point that can be inferred from the case material must be included. The case material may be very rich and provide more than enough points. The mark allocation is a good guide for how many points you actually need to include in your answer.

5.9.5 *"Discuss" questions with no clear thesis and anti-thesis*

Most "discuss" questions have a clear thesis and anti-thesis. However, that may not always be the case. For example, if we were to analyse the question "Discuss the factors that the Malaysian government should consider to determine whether to lift the movement control order (MCO)", we would notice that although the command word is "discuss", the content "the factors..." does not lend itself well to the development of a thesis and an anti-thesis.

At this point, some may be tempted to argue that the thesis is "the Malaysian government should lift the movement control order (MCO)" and the anti-thesis is "the Malaysian government should not lift the movement control order (MCO)". However, that would be a misinterpretation of the question. This set of thesis and anti-thesis answer the question "Discuss whether the Malaysian government should lift the movement control order (MCO)", which is an entirely different question.

Returning to the original question, "Discuss the factors that the Malaysian government should consider to determine whether to lift the movement control order (MCO)", what are we to do when the we observe a "discuss" question but cannot see any clear thesis or anti-thesis? The answer is simple — replace the word "discuss" with "explain". This would then make the points required for the body clear. For our example, this would mean that the question becomes "Explain the factors that the Malaysian government should consider to determine whether to lift the movement control order (MCO)". So, the points to be written could include the benefits of lifting the MCO such as the resumption of economic activity/growth as well as costs such as the possible spread of the coronavirus.

This leaves one problem unresolved — how can an evaluative conclusion be written when there's no thesis and anti-thesis to synthesise? There a few ways to solve this problem. One is to still synthesise all the points by ranking them in order of importance. For example, we could argue that of the factors that influence decisions (benefits, costs, constraints), constraints is the most important factor as it determines whether the decision is within the agent's choice set to begin with.

(*Continued*)

The other way to still earn the evaluation marks is to use evaluation approaches apart from synthesis (introduced near the start of this segment but reproduced below for your convenience):

- Evaluate critically, contemporary issues, perspectives and policy choices.
- Recognise unstated assumptions and evaluate their relevance.

So, using the question on discussing factors that the Malaysian government should consider to determine whether to lift the MCO as an example, one could conclude the answer by pointing out that the analysis of the benefits/costs made certain assumptions that may not hold in reality and how the analysis would change if the assumptions did not hold.

5.10 How to Answer a Question with Multiple Command Words

If there are multiple command words within a question, all you have to do is simply answer it as if it were two related questions. For example, if the question is "Suggest and explain a reason for the increase in the price of textiles", you could think of it as "Suggest a reason for the increase in the price of textiles" and "Explain how this reason caused an increase in the price of textiles". You can refer to the relevant sections in this chapter to see how to answer a "suggest" question and how to answer an "explain" question.

Some other examples of questions with multiple command words and how they can be broken up into part-questions are presented in Table 5.33.

The only thing you need to bear in mind is that the two part-questions are linked. For example, for the first question in Table 5.33, if you describe the trend as an increase in expenditure, then for the explanation, you must explain an increase in the expenditure. For the second example, if the reasons for the high youth unemployment are

Table 5.33: Breaking up questions with multiple command words into part-questions.

Question with Multiple Command Words	Part Questions
Describe the trend in the expenditure on organic meat and account for this trend.	• Describe the trend in the expenditure on organic food. • Account for (Explain) this trend.
Explain why Spain is facing "double-digit youth unemployment" and discuss the policies that the Spanish government may undertake to address it.	• Explain why Spain is facing "double-digit youth unemployment". • Discuss the policies that the Spanish government may undertake to address it.

structural and demand-deficient in nature, then the policies you discuss must be those that target structural and demand-deficient unemployment.

A further complication is that you do not know for sure how many marks are allocated to each part of the question. Nonetheless, in general, "discuss" questions carry more marks than "explain" questions, which in turn carry more marks than "describe"/"compare" questions so that should give you a rough sense of how much to write for each part.

5.10.1. *(H1 Economics 8843 syllabus only) How to answer the 6-mark "Comment" question*

The way to approach the 6-mark "comment" question is to first replace the "comment" with "explain". Then, answer the "explain" question to gain the first 4 marks. Next write an evaluative comment about your explanation to gain the last 2 marks. This evaluative comment about your explanation could be about the extent of the change explained, whether this change would persist in the long run, whether the explanation made any unstated assumptions, etc.

We illustrate the above using this 6-mark question as an example: "Comment on the increase in the price of pineapples (Extract 1)."

First, we would write an answer to the question "Explain the increase in the price of pineapples (Extract 1)." for the first 4 marks.

Then, to earn the last 2 marks, we might write something about the extent of the change in the price of pineapples being very large/small, or about whether we think this change in price will persist in the long run.

5.10.2 *Summary of how to answer case study questions*

This section summarises how to answer case study questions with different command words:

Command Word	How to Answer
Describe	Provide one description for each mark allocated. Descriptions can be: • Whether a balance is in surplus/deficit (for describing balances only) • Whether a relationship is direct/inverse (for describing relationships only) • General trend (overall increase/decrease) • Exceptions to the general trend • Sharpest changes in the same direction of the general trend • Rate of change
Compare	Provide one comparison for each mark allocated. Comparisons can be based on the following categories to determine whether there is a similarity or difference: • Comparing whether balance positions are in surplus or deficit (for comparing balances only) • Comparison of general trend (overall increase/ decrease)

(*Continued*)

(*Continued*)

Command Word	How to Answer
	• Comparison of extent of change (whether one changed more than other) • Comparison of levels (whether one was consistently higher than the other) • Comparison of rate of change (whether the changes in the two (or more) variables were at an increasing/decreasing rate) • Comparison of variance (whether one was fluctuating more than the other)
Calculate	Provide the relevant formula and show the calculation
Identify	Pick out what is required from the case material. Each mark allocated requires one thing to be identified
Suggest	Provide what is required based on theory or identify it from the case material Additional marks allocated imply that an explanation is needed too.
Infer/ Interpret	Include a brief explanation for each inference/interpretation For interpretation of elasticity values, both the sign as well as the magnitude should be interpreted and explained
Define	Reproduce the definition. Each term to be defined is one mark so additional marks allocated imply the need to provide something beyond a definition such as a formula or an example
*Explain	Step 1: Identify the cause-and-effect to be explained in the question Step 2: Unpack the effect in terms of economic variables (e.g., revenue = P × Q) Step 3: Determine the economic model to apply (e.g., to explain a change in P and/or Q, demand and supply model is needed) Step 4: Write out the answer by linking the cause to the economic model to the effect. Include diagrams if the question asks for it

(*Continued*)

Command Word	How to Answer

*Discuss	Planning stage:
	
	• Develop the thesis and anti-thesis
	• Select the points for inclusion from the case material and/or from theory (at least one point should be from the case material to avoid a purely theoretical answer if possible). A rule of thumb would be two substantial points for an 8m question and three for a 10m question
	• Plan for the evaluation by using the context to determine whether the thesis outweighs the anti-thesis (i.e., judgment with justification)
	
	Writing stage:
	
	• Introduction should be used to define key terms and provide background explanations if required
	• Each point in the body should be explained using economic models (as if each paragraph were answering an "explain" question). Draw diagrams to illustrate the points
	• For the conclusion, synthesis the thesis and anti-thesis by:
	  o Showing that the judgement depends on weighing the thesis against the anti-thesis points
	  o Showing that the context determines whether the thesis outweighs the anti-thesis
	  o Make a judgement based on the context (e.g., time period, state of the country/market, whether some factors can be/are mitigated by existing measures)

Note: *These two question types make up the majority of the marks in the case study question and should be prioritised in your revision.

References

Guerrero-López, C.M., Unar-Munguía, M., & Colchero, M.A. (2017). Price elasticity of the demand for soft drinks, other sugar-sweetened beverages and energy dense food in Chile. *BMC Public Health, 17*, 180. Retrieved on 23 May 2020 from: https://doi.org/10.1186/s12889-017-4098-x

Niemi, N. (2009). *The price elasticity of demand of fair trade coffee (Master's thesis)*. Helsinski: Helsinski School of Economics. Retrieved on 20 May 2020 from: http://epub.lib.aalto.fi/en/ethesis/pdf/12181/hse_ethesis_12181.pdf

Endnotes

1. More specifically, it is the class of verbs known as imperatives, but this is not a book about English grammar.
2. Do not worry if these measures sound unfamiliar to you. You will not need to use them in A Level Economics although you might need to know what they are for Mathematics.
3. Note that these are only approximations and not mathematically accurate although the true figures will not be very far off.
4. For the latest GCE A Level syllabuses for H1 and H2 Economics, refer to the Singapore Examinations and Assessment Board website. The syllabuses will be updated on an annual basis.

Part 2
Essay Skills

Chapter 6
Structure of the Essay Paper (For H2 Economics 9570 Syllabus)

To recap, for this syllabus, Paper 1 is the case study paper (which constitutes 40% of the total score) and Paper 2 is the essay paper (which constitutes the other 60%). Paper 2 is a 2-hour 15-minute paper where you will need to select 3 out of 6 essay questions to answer. The 6 essay questions are split into two sections — Section A contains 3 questions that predominantly test microeconomic concepts and Section B contains the other 3 questions that predominantly test macroeconomic concepts. At least 1 of the 3 questions that you select to answer must come from each section. This means that you must either answer 1 question from Section A and 2 questions from Section B or the other way around.

Additionally, each question is split into parts (a) and (b) where (a) would be a 10m "Explain" question and (b) would be a 15m "Discuss" question.

All above is summarised in Figure 6.1.

Figure 6.1: The structure of the H2 Economics Essay Paper.

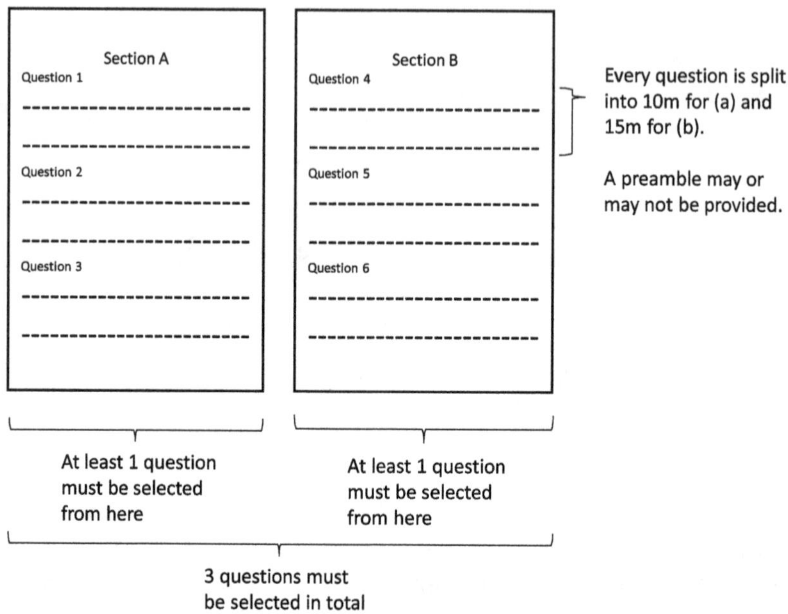

Chapter 7
Answering the Essay Questions

7.1 Question Selection — Which Questions to Answer?

Ideally, all the questions should be of equal difficulty. However, that does not always happen. So question selection becomes important. The main tip here is to:

- Select the "standard"/"easy" questions;

The logic is as follows. Some questions are "more standard" and you should choose those questions. This is because markers do not give bonus marks to candidates who select the difficult questions. Also, the marks are not normalised for each question before they are summed up, so a brilliant student who chooses the difficult questions could do worse than an average student who chooses the easier questions. We illustrate this with an example. Suppose we have two candidates — Candidate A and Candidate B. Candidate A chose a difficult question and scored 15/25 for it while everyone else who chose this question scored 10/25. Candidate B chose an easy question and scored 16/25 for it while everyone else who chose that question scored 21/25. Candidate B would still get a better grade than Candidate A (16 is more than 15) even though his answer was below average while Candidate A's was above average.

7.2 Analysing the Essay Questions

To determine which question is easier, you would need to analyse the questions to determine their requirements. Here too, the 3C+ framework for question analysis (explained in Chapter 5, Section 5.1.2) can be used. The summary of the 3C+ is reproduced below for your easy reference.

7.2.1 *Summary of the 3C+ framework*

In summary, the 3C+ framework refers to the identification of the:

3C+

The three "C"s are:
- Command word
- Content
- Context

"+" refers to additional condition(s)

- First "C" — Command word
  - This word tells you what to do (e.g., explain, discuss)
  - Every question must have at least one. Most questions have only one but it is possible for a question to have more.
- Second "C" — Content
  - This tells you what the command word is applied to
  - Can be identified by answering the question "(insert command word) what?"
  - Every command word must be applied to a piece of content
- Third "C" — Context
  - This usually tells you which market(s) to look at (for microeconomics) or which economy(s) to look at (for macroeconomics).
  - Not all essay questions have this
- "+" — Additional condition(s)
  - This gives you additional information/conditions to take note of
  - Some essay questions may have this but it is not often

7.3 Answering the Questions

Every essay question will always have the structure of a part (a) "explain" question and a part (b) "discuss" question.

We will work through an example to show the skills needed.

The sample question is:

The average price of surgical masks on e-retailing websites in the US rose by about 166% after the World Health Organisation (WHO) declared a global health emergency on Jan 30, 2020.

(a) Using demand and supply analysis, explain why the price of surgical masks rose so rapidly. [10]
(b) Discuss whether the US government should respond by capping the price of surgical masks. [15]

7.3.1 *Answering the 10m question*

Step 1: We analyse this question using the 3C+ framework:

- The command word is "explain". Similar to an "explain" question in a case study (Section 5.8 in Chapter 5), we would need to explain a cause-and-effect relationship.
- The content to be explained is "why the price of surgical masks rose so rapidly". In this case, the effect to be explained is a rapid increase in the price of face masks but the cause is not explicitly provided. One cause can be inferred from the preamble — WHO's declaration of a global health emergency. We will need to think of other causes in our planning stage. Additionally, the word "rapidly" tells us that we must not only explain the increase, but we must also explain why it is to such a large extent.
- The context is the US surgical mask market. So, other causes of the rapid rise in the price that we think of must be applicable to this market.

- The additional condition is "Using demand and supply analysis". This tells us the economic model we are to use. Even if this was not provided, we would have used this model anyway since we need to explain a change in price.

Step 2: We plan the answer. In planning, we want to make sure that our points have sufficient scope. This refers to having a range of points that show the breadth of understanding. For example, if the question is about explaining why a government should intervene in a market, then scope is shown from including explanations of different sources of market failure. Or, if the question is about reasons for inflation in a country, scope is shown from providing factors for demand-pull and cost-push inflation. Returning to our sample question, we may originally only see the following points:

- WHO declaring a global health emergency led to an increase in demand for surgical masks, which then caused the price to increase.
- The sharp increase in price may be due to masks having a price inelastic supply at the start of the pandemic as it takes time for machinery to be re-purposed to produce masks.

This does not provide sufficient scope since only a demand factor is provided (for questions requiring demand and supply analysis, scope is usually shown by explaining both demand and supply causes). As such, we may add on a supply factor that is applicable to the context.

- E-retailers may withhold the stocks of surgical masks in the current period as they might expect the price to increase in the future. This would cause the supply to fall.

Step 3: Once we have planned our points, we write out the answer. In writing out the answer, we:

- Include an introduction to define terms and provide the background.
- Provide detailed economic analysis for each of the points (to provide depth) in the body. For each of the points in the body, please

refer to Step 3 in Section 5.8.2 in Chapter 5 to see how to determine which economic model to apply (Table 5.26 in that section provides a good summary).

- Summarise the points for the conclusion. Note that for "explain" questions, there are no evaluation marks and a simple summary would suffice for the conclusion.

Introduction

The sharp rise in the price of surgical masks may be attributed to a rise in demand following WHO's declaration of a global health emergency, a price inelastic supply of surgical masks at that point in time, as well as a reduction in supply as US online retailers such as Amazon may have withheld stocks in anticipation of selling them at higher prices later.

Body I: Explain how the rise in demand from WHO's announcement caused price to increase

WHO's declaration would have caused consumers to react by buying surgical masks to protect themselves from the virus. This might also have been reinforced by some states in the US imposing mandatory mask-wearing in response to the WHO's announcement. Together, there would have been a rise in demand for surgical masks illustrated by the rightward shift of the demand curve from D_0 to D_1 in the figure below.

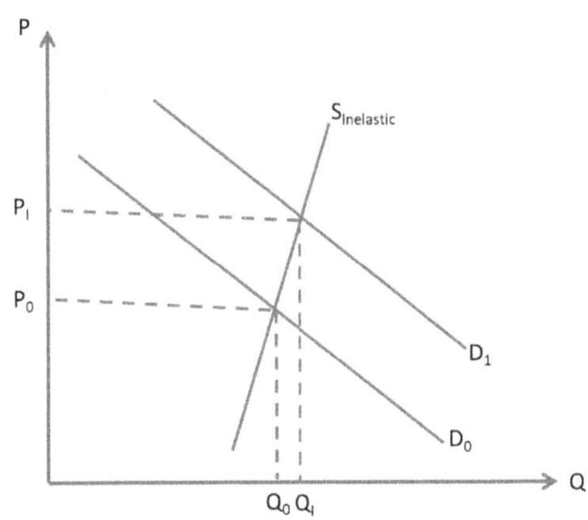

(*Continued*)

(Continued)

This increase in demand caused a shortage of surgical masks, which created an upward pressure on the price of surgical masks until it eventually rose from the original equilibrium price of P_0 to the new equilibrium price of P_1.

Body II: Explain how the low price elasticity of supply (PES) caused the extent of the increase in price to be large

Furthermore, the supply of face masks was likely to be price inelastic near the start of the pandemic when WHO made its announcement. This is because it takes time for machines to be repurposed to produce surgical masks and so in the short run, producers could not have responded to the increase in price by significantly increasing the quantity supplied. In other words, the increase in price would have only caused a less than proportionate increase in the quantity supplied of surgical masks. As such, the price would have increased by a lot before the shortage is cleared, causing a large rise in the price of surgical masks. This is illustrated in the earlier diagram where the steep supply curve caused the extent of the increase in price to be large.

Body III: Explain how the fall in supply from e-retailers withholding stocks caused price to increase

Additionally, US e-retailers such as Amazon might have anticipated that the price of surgical masks would rise following the announcement and might have responded by holding back stocks in anticipation of the higher price in the future. As such, the supply of surgical masks would have fallen, further adding to the shortage and hence further increasing the price.

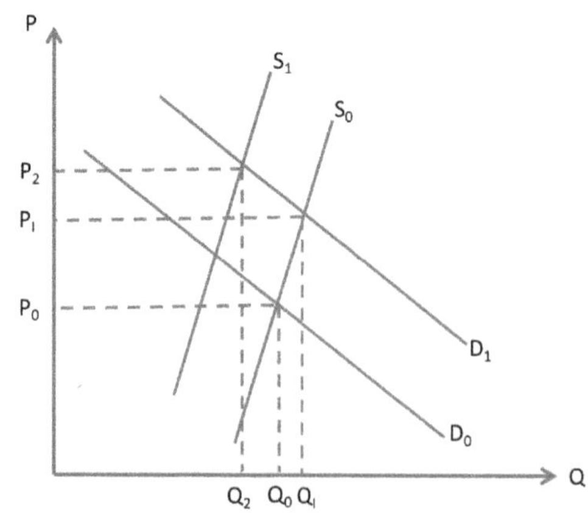

(*Continued*)

As can be seen from the diagram above, from the original equilibrium of P_0 and Q_0 where D_0 intersects S_0, the increase in demand caused the price to increase from P_0 to P_1 and the additional fall in supply from S_0 to S_1 caused the price to increase further from P_1 to P_2.

Conclusion: Summarise the points

In conclusion, the price of surgical masks increased rapidly because of the increase in demand due to WHO's announcements, the price inelastic supply of surgical masks, and the fall in supply from e-retailers withholding stocks.

7.3.2 *How a 10m question is marked*

While "explain" questions in the case study paper usually are no more than 6m, "explain" questions in essay papers are always 10m. As such, unlike "explain" questions in case studies which are marked by points (1m for each link in the explanation), "explain" questions in essays are marked by levels. Each level would have a set of descriptors and the answer would be read as a whole and placed in a level based on which descriptor it best matches. A level 1 answer would be 1–4 marks, a level 2 answer would be 5–7 marks, and a level 3 answer would be 8–10 marks. While the specific descriptors for the levels would vary from question to question, the descriptors for the highest level often contain the following elements:

- **Scope** — As mentioned in the earlier section, this refers to having a range of points that show the breadth of understanding. For example, if the question is about comparing the standard of living, then scope is shown from including comparisons of material and non-material aspects of standard of living. Or, if the question is about factors affecting unemployment, then scope is shown from including factors that affect demand-deficient, structural, and frictional unemployment.
- **Depth** — This refers to the use of economic analysis in the explanations. It usually involves using an economic model and reference to graphs.

- **Context** — This refers to inclusion of points relevant to the context given (assuming one is required). This is usually shown by providing relevant examples.

While individual rubrics will differ, they generally fall into this pattern:

Level	Descriptor	Mark Range
L3	Answer shows: • Scope • Depth • Context (assuming one is provided in the question)	8–10
L2	Answer shows: • Depth • Scope/context (assuming one is provided in the question) but not both	5–7
L1	Answer has no depth (i.e., a descriptive answer)	1–4

For our sample question specifically, the rubric will probably look something like this (words in italics to show the elements of scope, depth, and context):

Level	Descriptor	Mark Range
L3	An answer that that explains both demand and supply factors (*scope*) that could have contributed to the rise in the price of surgical masks (*context*). Well-labelled demand and supply diagrams are drawn and referenced to and relevant elasticity concepts are applied (*depth*).	8–10
L2	An answer that attempts to apply demand and supply analysis to explain the rise in the price of surgical masks. While relevant diagrams are drawn and referenced (*depth*), only a limited range of factors are considered (*lack of scope*).	5–7

(*Continued*)

Level	Descriptor	Mark Range
L1	An answer that attempts to explain the rise in the price of surgical masks. However, the answer is descriptive in nature (*lack of depth*).	1–4

As can be seen, depth is a key requirement as any answer without depth (i.e., does not use any economic analysis) would be stuck in L1 whereas the lack of scope/context (assuming context is required) still allows the answer to land in L2.

A common question that students wonder about is how many points to include. Rather than count the number of points, it is more important to ensure that the points used show sufficient scope. For example, in the sample that we did, an answer that explains three demand factors would score poorer than an essay that explains one demand factor and one supply factor. This is because the latter shows scope but the former does not.

Another common question is about how much detail to include. For this, we need to consider how many points are required. If the question requires two points (e.g., if a question requires explanations of factors provided in the preamble and there are two factors), then more detail should be provided (i.e., zoom in). However, if the question requires three points, then fewer details for each point are required (i.e., zoom out). A rule of thumb to follow would be for the length of the answer for part (a) to be approximately 1.5 pages long (including diagrams). The actual length would vary according to the size of the handwriting as well as how many diagrams are drawn of course.

A final point to note is that whether points beyond what is presented in the preamble can be included depends on the specific question phrasing. For example, if the question phrasing for the sample question had been "Explain how the above caused the price of surgical masks to rise so rapidly," then we could not have included the point on the fall in supply of surgical masks since that was not provided in the preamble. This is because the phrase "how the above" restricts us to only explain how the factor provided in the preamble caused the increase in the price of surgical masks.

7.3.3 *Answering the 15m question*

Like what we did for answering the 10m question, we will work through an example to show the skills needed to answer this type of question.

To recap, the sample question is:

The average price of surgical masks on e-retailing websites in the US rose by about 166% after the World Health Organisation (WHO) declared a global health emergency on Jan 30, 2020.

(a) Using demand and supply analysis, explain why the price of surgical masks rose so rapidly. [10]
(b) Discuss whether the US government should respond by capping the price of surgical masks. [15]

We now work through the answer for (b).

Step 1: We analyse this question using the 3C+ framework:

- The command word is "discuss". Similar to a "discuss" question in a case study (Section 5.9 in Chapter 5), we would need to write a thesis, anti-thesis, and an evaluation that synthesises the two.
- The content to be explained is "whether governments should respond by capping the prices of surgical masks". In this case, the thesis and anti-thesis would be:
  - The US government should respond by capping the price of surgical masks;
  - The US governments should not respond by capping the price of surgical masks.
- The context is the US government. So, our points should be applicable to the US.
- There are no additional conditions. So, we do not need to worry about this.

Step 2: We plan the answer. In planning, we want to make sure that we have both thesis and anti-thesis points, and that we have sufficient scope. To recap, scope refers to having a range of points that show the breadth of understanding. For our sample question, we know that whether a government should intervene in a market depends on whether a market achieves efficiency and equity. So, scope could be shown from using both efficiency and equity arguments in our answer. As such, our plan could be:

Thesis: The US government should respond by capping the price of surgical masks	**Anti-thesis:** The US governments should not respond by capping the price of surgical masks
• (Equity argument) Masks are necessities in a pandemic. Hence, the US government should cap the price to ensure affordability.	• (Equity argument) Price caps create shortages. As such, the poor may still not have access to surgical masks. Thus, the US government should not use price caps since better policies such as subsidies exist.
• Price caps cost the government less money and work faster than the alternatives (e.g., subsidies) subsidies in bringing prices down	• (Efficiency argument) Masks also generate positive externalities in reducing the risk of transmission. Price caps would create greater underconsumption. As such, the US governmnet should not use price caps since better policies such as subsidies exist.
Evaluation: Judgement must be about whether the US government should respond by capping the prices of surgical masks. This will depend on whether the thesis outweighs the anti-thesis (need to use context to determine this).	

In our selection of points, we intentionally chose points such that we would have points supporting the thesis and the anti-thesis, as well as points that show scope in terms of considering equity and efficiency.

Step 3: Once we have planned our points, we write out the answer. In writing out the answer, we:

- Include an introduction to define terms and provide the background.
- Provide detailed economic analysis for each of the points (to provide depth) in the body. We also organise the points so that there is a coherent flow.
- Synthesise the points for an evaluative conclusion. Similar to writing an evaluative conclusion for a "discuss question" in a case study, we want to make a judgement that answers the question and justify this judgement by synthesising the thesis and anti-thesis. A useful guide is to follow these steps:
    - Show that the judgement depends on weighing the thesis against the anti-thesis points;
    - Show that the context determines whether the thesis outweighs the anti-thesis;
    - Make a judgement based on the context.

A sample template would be:

"In conclusion, (the judgement to be made) would depend on the relative importance of (thesis and anti-thesis points). Given (insert the context), (the thesis points) would outweigh/be outweighed by (the anti-thesis points). As such, (make the judgement)."

However, there is one difference in writing an evaluation for a case study's "discuss" question and an essay's "discuss" question. For essays, there are 5m for evaluation whereas for case studies, the evaluation marks are only 2–3m. So, for essays, we should try to show how two or more aspects of the context will determine the judgement as opposed to just one. For our sample question, we will use the context of a pandemic as well as the US budget position to make our judgement.

<u>Introduction</u>

Capping prices means imposing a price ceiling on surgical masks that producers cannot price above. Whether the US government should do so in the market for surgical masks would depend on the nature of the market failure in the surgical mask market in the wake of the pandemic and also whether there are better policies available.

(*Continued*)

Body I: (Thesis) Explain how price caps would correct inequity

The US government should cap the price of surgical masks as the sharp rise in its price results in inequity. This is because equity requires that everyone have access to basic necessities regardless of income levels. In the Covid-19 pandemic, surgical masks provide protection and are hence necessities. However, the sharp rise in its price may cause the poor to be unable to afford this protection. This is inequitable as it is not morally right for someone to risk dying of a disease because of a lack of income. As such, the government should cap the price of such surgical masks to ensure affordability by all.

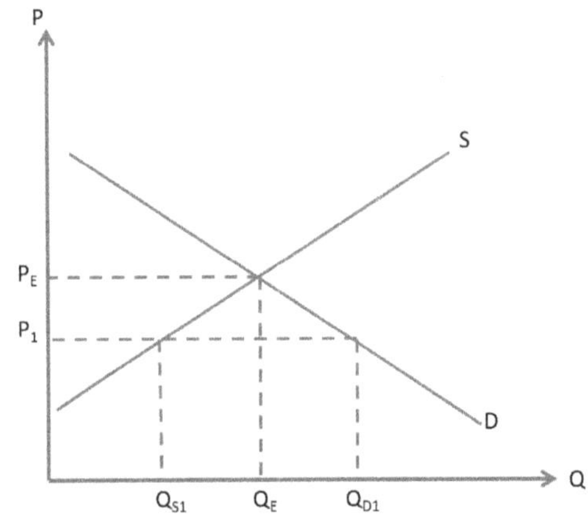

With reference to the diagram above, a price cap at the price P_1 would prevent prices from rising to P_E, ensuring affordability.

Body II: (Anti-thesis) Explain how price caps may not solve inequity due to the shortage created and how subsidies may be a better option

However, price caps lead to shortages as can be seen from the above diagram where quantity supplied falls to Q_{S1} and quantity demanded rises to Q_{D1}. Since quantity demanded exceeds quantity supplied, a shortage is formed. As such, even though the price is lower, many of the poor may still not have access to the surgical masks as they may not be lucky enough to get hold of the limited quantity supplied at P_1. In fact, it is likely that it will be the rich, who are able to hire people to monitor the e-retail

(*Continued*)

(*Continued*)

platforms to buy surgical masks once they are released on the market, who will get to consume the limited Q_{S1}.

As such, since price caps may not reduce inequity (at least, not significantly), the US government should not respond by capping prices. This is especially so when an alternative such as a subsidy can work better. A subsidy to surgical mask producers in the US would lower their cost of production and hence induce them to increase the supply.

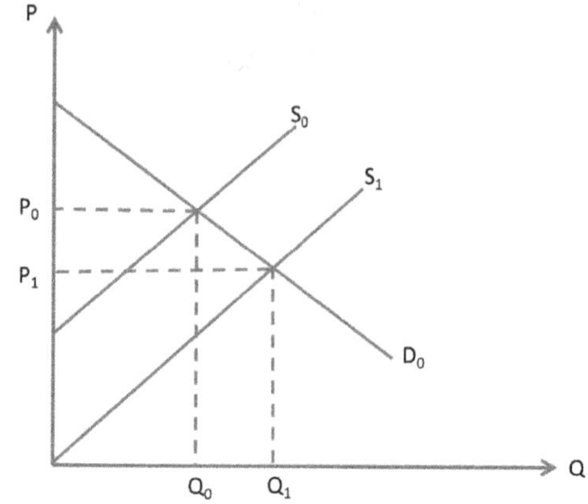

As seen from the diagram above, the increase in supply from S_0 to S_1 would help to lower prices from P_0 to P_1 and hence keep surgical masks affordable while not creating any shortage. In fact, even more masks can be consumed with the subsidy (from Q_0 to Q_1)

<u>Body III: (Anti-thesis) Explain how price caps may cause more inefficiency and how subsidies may be a better option</u>

Furthermore, price caps may worsen allocative inefficiency. In the pandemic, there are significant positive externalities in the consumption (i.e., use) of surgical masks as the use of such masks not only protect the individual from getting infected but also benefits third-parties in the form of lowering their risk of getting infected by the mask-wearer. Such marginal external benefit (MEB) causes the marginal social benefit (MSB) to diverge from the marginal private benefit (MPB) as MSB = MPB + MEB.

(*Continued*)

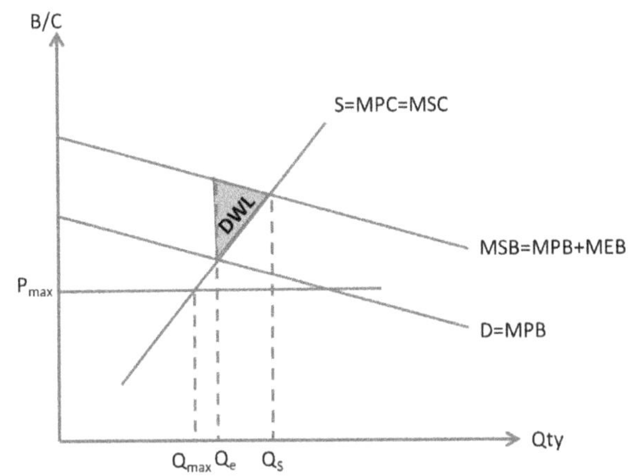

As can be seen from the diagram above, in the absence of government intervention, the market equilibrium would be at Qe where MPB = marginal private costs (MPC) as producers and consumers act in self-interests and only consider their private benefits and costs and ignore externalities. However, the social optimum is at Qs where MSB = marginal social costs (MSC). Since Qe is less than Qs, there is an underconsumption of face masks, creating a deadweight loss of the shaded area as MSB exceeds MSC for the quantities from Qe to Qs which are not produced/consumed.

A price cap at Pmax would worsen the problem by restricting production and hence consumption to Qmax, worsening the underconsumption and creating a larger deadweight loss.

In contrast, a subsidy (assuming that it is equal to MEB) would increase the supply of masks and cause the market equilibrium quantity to increase from Qe to Qs as shown in the diagram below.

As such, because of the differing effects on allocative efficiency, it may be better for the US government to not respond by capping the price of surgical masks but to subsidise mask production instead.

(*Continued*)

(*Continued*)

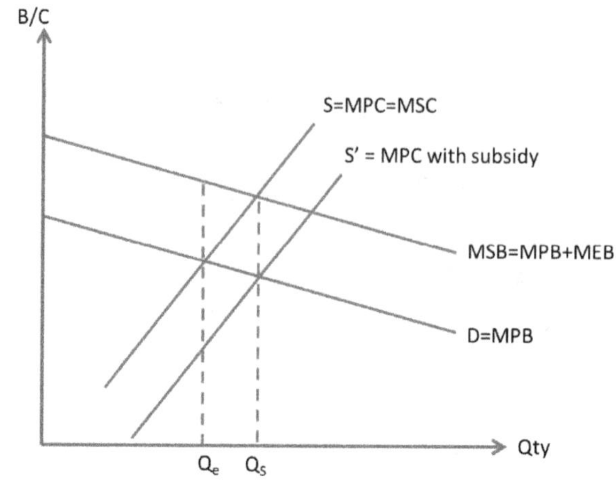

Body III: (Thesis) Explain how price caps may still be the best option because it may cost less and show effects faster.

Nonetheless, there are still some advantages to price caps to consider. Price ceilings may cost the US government less money compared to subsidies since subsidies need to be funded. While the enforcement of a price ceiling would require the US government to incur some monitoring and enforcement costs, such costs may be relatively low since prices by e-retailers are online and can be fairly easily monitored. Further, assuming the legislation passes quickly, a price ceiling would have an almost immediate effect on the price of surgical masks whereas subsidies will take more time to work as producers need time to ramp up production.

Conclusion: Make a judgement and justify it

In conclusion, whether the US government should cap the price of surgical masks in response to the increase in its price would depend on the relative importance of reducing inequity, reducing inefficiency, balancing the government budget, and having a policy that works quickly. For the reduction of inequity and inefficiency, subsidies do a better job than price ceilings whereas for balancing the government budget (or at least not worsening the deficit too much) and having a policy that has an immediate effect, price ceilings are preferred. Given the context of a severe pandemic, the need for a policy that has immediate effects is large and in that sense, the

(*Continued*)

speed at which a price ceiling works would be a crucial advantage. Furthermore, given US's context of having large government deficits, the impact on the government budget is an important consideration too. As such, the US government should cap the prices of surgical masks in the short run to buy time for them to reallocate spending (so that the budget position will not worsen) towards subsidies that work better in the longer term.

7.3.4 *How a 15m question is marked*

"Discuss" questions in a case study and in an essay are similar in that they are both marked by levels and have marks set aside for evaluation. Each level would have a set of descriptors and the answer would be read as a whole and placed in a level based on which descriptor it best matches. However, a "discuss" question in a case study would only be 8m or 10m while a part (b) "discuss" question in an essay is 15m. As such, there are a few differences:

- "Discuss" questions in case studies have only two levels of marks while 15m "discuss" questions in essays have three levels.
- "Discuss" questions in case studies carry only 2–3 evaluation marks while 15m "discuss" questions in essays carry 5 evaluation marks.

As such, the demand for a 15m "discuss" question in an essay is higher. While the specific descriptors for the levels would vary from question to question, the descriptors for the highest level often contain the following elements (you will notice that there is an additional element compared to the descriptor for "discuss" questions for case studies in Section 5.9.1 of Chapter 5):

- **Balance** — This refers to having both a thesis and an anti-thesis. For instance, if the question is "Discuss whether the Federal Reserve should raise interest rates", then the thesis would be "The Federal Reserve should raise interest rates" and the anti-thesis would be "The Federal Reserve should not raise interest rates". An answer would only be balanced if it includes points for both the thesis and the anti-thesis.

- **Scope** — As mentioned in the earlier section on how "explain" essays are marked, this refers to having a range of points that show the breadth of understanding. For example, if the question is about comparing the standard of living, then scope is shown from including comparisons of material and non-material aspects of standard of living. Or, if the question is about factors affecting unemployment, then scope is shown from including factors that affect demand-deficient, structural, and frictional unemployment.
- **Depth** — This refers to the use of economic analysis in the explanations. It usually involves using an economic model and reference to graphs.
- **Context** — This refers to inclusion of points relevant to the context given (assuming one is required). This is usually shown by providing relevant examples.

While individual rubrics will differ, they generally fall into this pattern:

Level	Descriptor	Mark Range
L3	Answer shows: • Balance, • Scope, • Depth, • Context (assuming one is provided in the question).	8–10
L2	Answer shows: • Depth, • Balance/scope/context (assuming one is provided in the question) but not all three.	5–7
L1	Answer has no depth (i.e., a descriptive answer).	1–4
	For evaluation	
E3	For a judgement that answers the question. Justification is provided and fully developed.	4–5

(*Continued*)

Level	Descriptor	Mark Range
E2	For a judgement that answers the question. Justification is provided but not fully developed.	2–3
E1	For a judgement that answers the question but with no/an unconvincing justification.	1

For our sample question specifically, the rubric will probably look something like this (words in italics to show the elements of balance, scope, depth, and context):

Level	Descriptor	Mark Range
L3	An answer that that makes the case for and against the US government imposing a price ceiling in response to the increase in the price of face masks (*balance and context*). Arguments raised made use of relevant economic concepts (*scope*) and were explained with the aid of well-labelled diagrams (*depth*).	8–10
L2	An answer that attempted to make a case for and/or against the US government imposing a price ceiling in response to the increase in the price of face masks (*may or may not be balanced*). While relevant diagrams are drawn and referenced (*depth*), only a limited range of factors are considered (*lack of scope*).	5–7
L1	An answer that attempts to make a case for and/or against the US government imposing a price ceiling in response to the increase in the price of face masks (*may or may not be balanced*). However, the answer is descriptive in nature (*lack of depth*).	1–4

(*Continued*)

(*Continued*)

Level	Descriptor	Mark Range
	For evaluation	
E3	For a judgement about whether the US government should impose a price ceiling in response to the increase in the price of face masks. Justification is provided and fully developed.	4–5
E2	For a judgement about whether the US government should impose a price ceiling in response to the increase in the price of face masks. Justification is provided but not fully developed.	2–3
E1	For a judgement about whether the US government should impose a price ceiling in response to the increase in the price of face masks but with no/an unconvincing justification.	1

As can be seen, depth is a key requirement as any answer without depth (i.e., does not use any economic analysis) would be stuck in L1 whereas the lack of balance/scope/context (assuming context is required) still allows the answer to land in L2.

A common question that students wonder about is how many points to include. Rather than count the number of points, it is more important to ensure that the points used show balance and scope. For example, in the sample that we did, an answer that makes two arguments in favour of the thesis and two arguments in favour of the anti-thesis but only considers inequity would score poorer than an essay that explains two arguments in favour of the thesis and one argument in favour of the anti-thesis but considers both inequity and inefficiency in the process. This is because the latter shows scope but the former does not. A similar line of thinking applies to balance — an unbalanced essay with more points will score poorer than a balanced essay with fewer points.

Another common question is about how much detail to include. A rule of thumb to follow would be for the length of the answer for part (b) to be approximately 2.5 pages (including diagrams). The actual length would vary according to the size of the handwriting as well as how many diagrams are drawn of course. If you can only think of two points, then make up for it by providing more detail.

Finally, below are some tips for writing the evaluation (these are similar to the tips for writing the evaluation for case study "discuss" questions since the skills are similar):

- Very seldom are there "correct" conclusions. Two opposite conclusions could be equally valid. What matters is making sure your thought process is clearly explained and not so much what conclusion you reach. Of course, factually wrong assumptions about the context (e.g., if you assume that the Covid-19 pandemic is just a minor inconvenience) would be penalised.
- If you do not have information about the context given (e.g., if you do not know whether the US fiscal position is healthy), then explain what information/data you would need and how you would use this information/data to make a judgement (e.g., "Furthermore, we would need to collect information on US debt to GDP ratio to determine how healthy their fiscal position is. If this ratio is high, the impact on the government budget would be an important consideration and price ceilings may be a better choice. Conversely, if it is low, then price ceilings may not be the better choice".
- If the question does not specify a context (e.g., if the question had been "Discuss whether governments should cap the prices of surgical masks.", explain that the judgement would depend on the context and bring in a specific country's/market's context as an example of what the judgement would be for that context (e.g., "In conclusion, whether any government should cap the price of surgical masks depends on the relative importance of reducing inequity, reducing inefficiency, balancing the government budget, and having a policy that works quickly for that country. For example, for the US...".

A final point to note is that given the tight timeline (3 essays to be written in 2 h 15 min) and the amount of effort it takes to get to E3, it is usually better to aim to write three essays that all land in L3 and E2 (minimally 54 marks) than to write two essays that land in L3 and E3 but run out of time for the third essay (maximum of 50 marks). In short, it is not wise to chase the last two evaluation marks. A judgement and some sort of justification will do.

7.4 Answering "Discuss" Questions with No Clear Thesis or Anti-thesis

In essays, as with case studies, you may encounter "discuss" questions with no clear thesis or anti-thesis. The way to deal with such questions is reproduced below from the case study section for your easy reference.

An example of a "discuss" question with no clear thesis or anti-thesis is "Discuss the factors that the Malaysian government should consider to determine whether to lift the movement control order (MCO)." We would notice that although the command word is "discuss", the content "the factors..." does not lend itself well to the development of a thesis and an anti-thesis.

At this point, some may be tempted to argue that the thesis is "the Malaysian government should lift the movement control order (MCO)" and the anti-thesis is "the Malaysian government should not lift the movement control order (MCO)". However, that would be a misinterpretation of the question. This set of thesis and anti-thesis answer the question "Discuss whether the Malaysian government should lift the movement control order (MCO)", which is an entirely different question.

Returning to the original question, "Discuss the factors that the Malaysian government should consider to determine whether to lift the movement control order (MCO)", what are we to do when the we observe a "discuss" question but cannot see any clear thesis or anti-thesis? The answer is a simple trick — replace the word "discuss" with "explain". This would then make the points required for the body clear. For our example, this would mean that the question becomes "Explain the factors that the Malaysian government should consider to determine whether to lift the movement control order (MCO)". So, the points to be written could include the benefits of lifting the MCO such as the resumption of economic activity/growth as well as costs such as the possible spread of the Corona virus.

This leaves one problem unresolved — how can an evaluative conclusion be written when there's no thesis and anti-thesis to synthesise? There a few ways to solve this problem. One is to still synthesise all the points by ranking them in order of importance. For example, we could argue that of the factors that influence decisions (benefits, costs, constraints), constraints is the most important factor as it determines whether the decision is within the agent's choice set to begin with.

The other way to still earn the evaluation marks is to use evaluation approaches apart from synthesis:

- Evaluate critically contemporary issues, perspectives and policy choices.
- Recognise unstated assumptions and evaluate their relevance.

So, using the question on discussing factors that the Malaysian government should consider to determine whether to lift the MCO as an example, one could conclude the answer by pointing out that the analysis of the benefits/costs made certain assumptions that may not hold in reality and how the analysis would change if the assumptions did not hold.

7.4.1 *Summary of skills to answer essay questions*

This section summarises the skills to answer essay questions. 10m questions are always "explain" questions and 15m questions are always "discuss" questions. You will notice that there are basically only two types of command words ("explain" and "discuss") and hence only two sets of skills.

Command Word	Skills
Explain	Step 1: Analyse the question using the 3C+. Step 2: Plan the answer — ensure points show scope and context. Step 3: Write the answer: Intro — define terms and establish background. Body — use economic analysis whenever possible to show depth. Graphs and references to graphs always help. Conclusion — summarise.
Discuss	Step 1: Analyse the question using the 3C+ Step 2: Plan the answer — ensure points show balance, scope, and context Step 3: Write the answer: Intro — define terms and establish background. Body — use economic analysis whenever possible to show depth. Graphs and references to graphs always help. Conclusion — evaluate by making a judgement and justify that judgement by using the context.

Chapter 8
Tips for Answering Unusual Questions

In this last chapter, we provide some tips for answering unusual questions. Unusual questions are questions where the question requirement is not immediately clear. For example, we know that "explain" questions normally require an explanation of cause-and-effect, however, you may also come across questions such as "Explain the relevance of the concept of elasticities in determining the relative tax burdens of an indirect tax." For this question, the cause and the effect are not immediately clear. However, if we analyse it more closely, we can think of the cause as a higher/lower PED or PES value and the effect as a larger/smaller tax burden on consumers and producers. This gives us our first tip — (for explain questions) if the cause and effects are not immediately clear, read it more closely.

If the question is still unclear, then at the start of your answer, write down your interpretation of the question. For example, in this case, we could interpret the question as "Explain how a high PED and low PES would affect consumers' and producers' tax burdens." Then, answer the question based on your interpretation. If your interpretation is not too far off, you would still earn some marks.

The next tip is to remember that definitions of economic terms and economic analysis will usually earn you some marks. So, minimally, define the terms that you can and if you can identify what topic the question is from (for our example, it is clearly from the topic on elasticities), try to do some related analysis. For this case, we might at least draw a diagram to illustrate relative tax burdens.

The last (but perhaps most important) tip is that if you can avoid the unusual question (i.e., if the unusual question is an essay question in the H2 Economics paper which you can choose not to do), avoid it. If it is unavoidable because it is a case study question, then give it your best shot and move on. Do not waste time agonising over it.

Index

www.ingramcontent.com/pod-product-compliance
Lightning Source LLC
LaVergne TN
LVHW011813200926
848484LV00005B/1182
9789811274787